Life & Love Lessons

How to Discover Confidence Through Your Spiritual Journey

MELINDA VAN FLEET

Copyright 2021 by Melinda Van Fleet, Two Adirondacks LLC
Thriving Communication Press™

All rights reserved. This publication or any portion may not be reproduced, distributed, or used in any manner without the written consent of the publisher and author. Limited use, giving credit to the author in quotations, is allowed. Anything more than that, email the author for permission.
info@melindavanfleet.com

Disclaimer: Publisher and author are not responsible for any personal (mental or medical) experiences, loss, or results. Results may vary and are based on individual's desire for success and therein actions taken. The content is based on the author's personal experience and will not be held liable.

Special thank you to my editor-Valerie Costa of Costa Creative Services
Contact at valerie@costacreativeservices.com

Library of Congress Number 2021912026
ISBN 978-1-7365917-3-4 Book
ISBN 978-1-7365917-4-1 eBook
ISBN 978-1-7365917-5-8 Audible

Cover Design by 100Covers.com
Interior Design by FormattedBooks.com

edication

This book, which comes from a heart-centered place of gratitude, is written for all the beautiful souls awakened to life's potential or are in the awakening process.

I didn't hold back in sharing my stories in the spirit that you don't hold back in your life.

Confidently—
Melinda

This book, which comes from a heart-centered place of gratitude, is written for all the beautiful souls awakened to life's potential or are in the awakening process.

I didn't hold back in sharing my stories in the spirit that you don't hold back in your life.

Confidently—
Melinda

Contents

Foreword vii
Preface xi
Introduction xvii

Chapter 1   Dipping My Toe… 1
Chapter 2   The Smoothie 7
Chapter 3   Spiritual Hobby 11
Chapter 4   Discovering Kabbalah 15
Chapter 5   The Tarot Card Reading that Changed Everything ... 21
Chapter 6   Bread Crumbs 35
Chapter 7   The Power of "What If" 51
Chapter 8   Your Soul's Journeys 59
Chapter 9   Why Can't They? 65
Chapter 10 Obsessed with Human Design 71
Chapter 11 I Give Myself Permission 79
Chapter 12 The Vision Board Quest 85
Chapter 13 Money is Energy 91

Chapter 14	Every day, I am Learning	101
Chapter 15	Celebration and Gratitude	107
Chapter 16	Sending Good Thoughts	113
Chapter 17	Time and Letting Go	123
Chapter 18	Guidance from the Other Side	133
Chapter 19	When am I Going to Listen?	139
Chapter 20	Who Am I?	147

Acknowledgments 149

Foreword

Melinda and I met in a mastermind group and clicked from the start. Since then I've had the honor of reading her Akashic Records Soul Blueprint to help maximize her innate gifts. I've also had the privilege of being a guest on her podcast a number of times. Along the way she's become a trusted friend and invaluable sounding board.

I feel blessed to know and have Melinda in my life. So when she asked me to write the foreword for her book it was an instant yes. The opportunity to shine a spotlight on her as the amazing empowered woman and entrepreneur I know is an honor and delight.

As I read *Life & Love Lessons*, I am struck with the way Melinda simplifies and demystifies manifesting, weaving it seamlessly throughout her stories. For her manifesting is a way of life, as natural as breathing.

How many times have you tried to follow some guru's guidance on manifesting only to end up even more frustrated? In this book, Melinda fills in the details that are missing from so many other teachings. *Life & Love Lessons* is practically a Law Of Attraction instruction manual. That's a huge bonus on top of all the other lessons she shares!

Imagine hurtling downhill at breakneck speed, certain you're going to crash. Most people reflexively assume the fetal position (or as close as possible), then remain frozen, bracing for the inevitable.

If you're Melinda, crashing isn't a consideration. She will calmly downshift, assess the situation, chart a new course, then shift into overdrive, manifesting a new outcome, all the while laughing with joy.

Shhh…I'll let you in on a little secret: If you want to score points with Melinda, admire her puppies and compliment her husband. That will surely earn you a ton of goodwill. A girl's got to have her priorities. 😊

One of the things I especially admire about Melinda is her ability to calmly work through challenges to find a winning solution. She's genius at analyzing a problem, reconfiguring her mindset, and obliterating the obstacle. Like the story about…oh wait, I don't want to give it away, you'll find the details further on in these pages.

In this book you'll discover a great many powerful and practical life lessons that could be exactly the answer you've been searching for.

When it comes to relationships that's where Melinda's super power shines. In these days when so many relationships fail, Melinda and Ryan are an inspirational success story. They've worked through challenges that would have flattened others to create a solid partnership where both thrive. They are each other's biggest cheerleaders and supporters. A testament to how it can be, if you're willing to put in the effort and make the commitment. I can think of no one better to consult if you want to create more successful relationships, both personal and professional.

When Melinda says she's a Peak Performance & Confidence Coach, that's not hyperbole. In Melinda's world it makes no sense to take a half-baked approach. If it's worth doing, it's worth going all out to reach your goal, experience more confidence and more satisfaction. Then it's on to the next challenge. When she sets a goal, there's no question she'll achieve it. No regrets, no excuses. I really admire that about her.

When it comes to work, Melinda is as serious as a heart attack. What makes her so remarkable is she also knows the importance of, and honors the need, to let her hair down and play to maintain the equilibrium vital for living the dream.

The hallmark of an excellent coach is one who uses lessons from their own life to more powerfully enlighten and engage their clients. No holds barred. That's the kind of power coach you want on your side on your path to success. That's my friend Melinda.

Debbra Lupien, Voice of the Akashic Records
Int'l Bestselling Author of *Akasha Unleashed: The Missing Manual to You*

Preface

> "The secret of change is to focus all of your energy not on fighting the old, but on building the new."
> —Socrates

Why? Why did I write this book?

It's interesting to understand the why behind what you do.

Why is that (pun intended)? Because understanding your why is one way to help keep you motivated and on track in anything you do. As an author, why am I writing this book? As a reader, why are you reading this book? It's a thought process as old as the hills, which means it's important. But the majority of the world goes through each day operating on autopilot.

Besides knowing why, I also layered in intention when I started to become immersed in studying and applying more spiritual tools in my life.

According to Wikipedia, intention is:

A mental state that represents a commitment to carrying out an action or actions in the future.

The callout here of the mental state is important. We can all immerse ourselves and focus on what we need to do, but until we understand what we are thinking and why, and move forward in adjusting our mental state, changes may not occur.

And only you can recognize your mental state. Change is a mental game.

It's work, which is why many people do not change or move forward in their lives.

You have also probably heard a zillion times before (no joke), "Change starts with you." But for most people, they repost a saying, like about change, on Instagram or Facebook, and move one. They never really know what the heck it means or do something about it.

What I have come to experience over the years is an innate knowing of things, but not quite the utmost clarity on piecing it together to confirm my intuition or the direction on which to take. If you follow me, you know I am an action taker. Good or bad, I take action and move forward. Often, I have to pivot or change something which may cause a setback, but it's how I work. I am by Human Design a Generator. Since learning this, I have made some serious changes to how I take action. The importance of learning my design type is something I will refer to on and off throughout this book journey.

Spiritual tools, teachers, and lessons have come in handy in helping me to gain clarity and continuing to make changes and move forward. I thrive on being able to take action. I have to practice not taking action. Using more feminine energy has always been my weakest trait.

In full transparency, I also have to work on busting through other people's judgment on how it is best advised in their expert opinion which direction to take. I had a conversation along those lines yesterday regarding a course. I've also had to stop listening to others and learn to trust my intuition. I have had to learn to protect myself against negative statements and other people's opinions. It's not always easy; however, it is crucial. And when you master the mental state of that new being and doing, it feels good.

There is no black, white, or perfection. Only what makes you feel good. Truth.

This book will weave a lot of tools, teachers, and topics throughout because like our lives, they all intertwine. What's the cotton commercial from Cotton Incorporated? "The fabric of our lives." People may have varying opinions about the message's relevance, but it was a jingle that stuck and came to my mind as I was typing this. All the threads make up the fabric of our lives. But again, to circle back, we often don't take time to recognize all the threads because we are on autopilot.

I can never express enough how important it is to appreciate our time on this Earth and to maximize our potential. Whether you are someone who makes annual business goals or plans a vacation, both are significant because you are making use of your time for something you desire. I have heard some coaches go back and forth on goal planning because the theory is that if you don't hit your goals, you may become disappointed and stuck. I can see someone falling into that pattern. But a goal can help you make good use of your time, so I think the reward may outweigh the risk.

As you read through this book, I intend to share what I have learned and how the learnings intertwine so you may pick up some helpful ideas. Or maybe you have had various readings, worked with teachers and coaches, and didn't connect the dots on how the insights can help. You may have even forgotten about a reading you had a few years ago. If you take notes or record the calls like I do, go back and listen. You may be amazed at what has transpired in that time. I have been amazed on several occasions by how something has shifted or transpired. I bet you will be, too.

I will also go back and forth mentioning some people as well as gifts if they intertwine.

This book is a weaved story timeline to show how your spiritual journey can come together through various tools, tips, and, most importantly, spiritual teachers. I don't know where I would be without those teachers. I like to think of myself as a vessel, and I love sharing their unique gifts.

I have a strong intuition, but I don't possess the majority of the gifts I will be sharing, at least not at this moment. I have felt called to write this book for a long time now, and the stories, lessons, guidance, and tools keep coming. It was finally time to put a date on the calendar and do the thing! Write the book!

So, I am over the moon pleased to share so many fabulous stories and ideas which I hope will help you, as well. I may zig-zag a little bit and themes may resurface. The timing may be off for some for what I share with you, but you can revisit this book when you are stuck and need a new idea on how to move forward. For various reasons, not all names are mentioned, but I still wanted to share the story.

Some people we meet on our journey serve a purpose for a short time, but then it's okay to move on. Energetically, it's my story and that makes me feel good. I wish that same positive energy and awareness about setting boundaries to feel good for you, as well.

What I also want to get across is we all have different experiences and beliefs. Our differences make the world go round. You may agree or disagree with something I write, and to me, that's cool. I don't feel I am set in stone, so it will be interesting to me to go back and read this in a few years' time and see how I feel. And that's important—feel.

I don't put any of these tools or teachings on such a high pedestal that it takes away from how I feel. I roll along, trying new tools and readings and applying them. If something doesn't feel good, I move on. I would hope anyone else reading this book has the same perspective. Look at this book as something interesting to read; enjoyable, easy, and to the point, and if you pick up a few tips, tools or a-ha moments, that's fabulous. I had the same mindset when I was writing *Confidence Mastery for Couples* (also referred to as CMFC).

I remember asking my good friend and spiritual teacher Debbra Lupien, who I will reference on and off throughout this book, "Am I a tarot/psychic junkie because I like to have readings?"

I felt a bit ashamed and embarrassed that I had three readings within a month's time, and wondered if I had an issue. Debbra assured me, "No, because you take action and apply the learnings." *Whew! Thank you, Debbra!*

If you collect Tarot/Oracle cards, are you using them and applying the insights you receive? Or are they collecting dust on your shelves? If you are reading this going, "Yep, that's me," grab a deck and see what pops out. I would love to hear what energy was brought out in the card you pulled.

That's the golden ticket! Feeling good! I will mention some other golden tickets throughout. Just think *Willie Wonka and The Chocolate Factory*. How amazing that Charlie and his grandpa found the golden ticket and how the story manifested. When you watched it way back when (at least if you are my age), you likely had no idea what manifesting was, right?

Master some of these golden tickets along with positive energy, mindset shifts, and crushing triggers and you will see results. (I have the chills now…thank you guides!)

Let's begin…

> "Make the journey as magical as the destination."
> —Bella Luna

Introduction

Saturday, March 6, 2021

> "Your wings already exist, all you have to do is fly."
> —Unknown.

It's three days until the launch of my first book as a solo author —*Confidence Mastery for Couples (CMFC)*.

I am excited, a bit nervous and at the same time feeling the itch to move forward.

I know…I should be a normal person and continue to focus on all I need to be doing for the first book—I call it the P's:

- Promotion
- Pitching (trying to get on TV—we will see what happens)
- Pinterest—need to focus more on Pinterest

BUT! If I am to live my life with joy and ease, I feel like starting this book.

This book has been percolating longer than I can account. There are moments when I feel my skin is on fire, I have chills, my brain is about to burst, or I am about to burst into tears. It's the weirdest feeling. I have so much to share with these stories and have learned so much over the years that I doubt I would be where I am as a human if I didn't acknowledge or use the tools and gifts which have been given to me along the way.

Even the fact that I took my computer outside to start to type this goes back to guidance. I had been told in many readings, "You need to get outside more. Get grounded in the earth." I listened, learned and am now remembering to apply guidance from the Universe.

Further than going outside to type this, I am also envisioning our breathtakingly beautiful backyard, our soon-to-be gorgeous porch overlooking the ocean, our fabulous pool with waterfalls and a big Buddha statue. While in all reality, our current backyard is kind of dumpy. I have made the best of it, but it won't be photographed in *Coastal Living* anytime soon.

If you have been following me, you know that I have manifested some amazing things in my life. I use story share to get these concepts I have learned across to you, the reader. My intention is that you see the results and know the potential, or are reminded. Often, we get busy in our day-to-day life and forget how powerful our mind is.

I have manifested:

- Amazing jobs with big companies
- Living by "the blue bridge" in downtown Chicago (now it's a white bridge)
- Living in NYC
- My husband, Ryan
- Moving to the Florida Keys and our charter business Good Karma Sportfishing
- And even our cute little dog Stella

To name a few…

Everything I share in this book has helped me build confidence and I intend to share that insight with you.

You can change your life. You can improve your thoughts, beliefs, feelings, energy—all the things.

And this book is proof.

I hope you enjoy it!

The chills right now are crazy! Thank you guides for helping me get this all out.

Love to everyone.

Chapter 1
Dipping My Toe...

WHEN DID I REALIZE I could make things come true? I had no idea that there was a whole methodology or science to making things come true. But! I did believe in the Ouija board.

I still have a Ouija board in our hallway closet. Ryan never wants to play with me.

My grandma on my mom's side was the one who introduced me to the Ouija board. She and I would sit in the dark basement and ask questions. I wasn't scared and I believed the answers from the board.

I remember her asking the Ouija when my grandpa would retire and the piece moved. I thought it was so cool. I remember asking what my husband's name would be, and it said, Matthew. Matthew is my husband Ryan's middle name. *Close, but no cigar.*

I remember it fondly and I remember my grandma being "on the money" with many things. Callouts about my behavior, how people looked at me and treated me. How my shoplifting arrest at age 19 had stemmed from my mother and her spending habits. And even when I met my husband Ryan, she knew right away that he was the one who I was going to marry.

My grandma told me, "You are two peas in a pod and will get married."

Even though I would not call my grandma a true psychic or even someone who openly shared her gift, it was my first taste of magic and that there was some higher power or "knowing."

You know, back then we didn't have the internet. Now, so many tools, teachers and information are at our fingertips. We are so lucky; especially the younger generation. I have spent time with my 15-year-old niece, Sienna, sharing a lot of the things I have learned so far. It's been fun to share conversations with Sienna about crystals, the moon phases, psychics, journaling, tarot and oracle cards and how she has potential and a team to help her. If I only knew those things at her age, I would likely be farther ahead in this lifetime.

But then, this is my soul path and journey.

And that is my niece's, which I celebrate and cheer her on!

Now, at age 50 (woo hoo!) I feel so excited to share vs. hide. I don't give a rat's ass if someone thinks I am crazy, loo loo, making stuff up, delusional or any other words or judgments they may have.

I feel they are missing out on not taking advantage of the gifts the universe gives us. And if you are someone that doesn't have the belief system, that's okay, because not everyone does, which is part of the journey.

Have you ever heard the words Star Seeds? Star Seeds are souls that are from another universe, hence the attraction to the metaphysical and anything spiritual. If someone is not attracted to these types of things, it likely means that their soul is from Earth.

What is amazing about this is that it is nothing we can control, right? So, if someone doesn't believe you, see your point of view or have interest, it's likely their soul is from Earth. Love them and move along.

Whew! What an amazing amount of pressure to release. Some people advise not to share your beliefs with others for fear of not being believed. Share what you feel like sharing, what calls to you and roll with it. I highly doubt many people who are from Earth will gravitate to this book, and that's okay.

I have read and talked to a lot of people that had some sort of spiritual awakening as a child. Then they move on into their early adult years and either block it or forget about it. Then it appears again. I had this experience, as well. Fast forward to my late twenties, which is where it all began again.

I lived in NYC. I was lonely and desperately wanting a boyfriend. I write about my boyfriend journey regarding the mega church in *Confidence Mastery for Couples (CMFC)*.

The desire for a boyfriend, prior to the megachurch, led me to a very pricey psychic smack dab in the middle of the Big Apple. I can visualize exactly where her space is and could even probably find it if I went back and tried. She was expensive, but at the time, in my desperation, I didn't care. I had a good job, so money wasn't an issue.

The psychic told me that my past lives were holding me back and I needed to clear some of that karma by carrying a black spool of thread tucked into my underwear every day. Yes, *you read that correctly.*

I also needed to call her on the phone so that she could light candles in my favor.

Hum...what the hell, why not? I did it. And...no boyfriend. I waited for him to magically appear, but nope. Nothing.

I consistently tried to call her, but she was hard to reach. I gave her grace. When I did finally reach her, she wanted me to pay her more money and switch to carrying $1,000 cash in my underwear. I remember clarifying the direction as I was so dumbstruck that this was actually something someone was telling me to do. *First a spool of thread, now hard cold cash? Really? Is this a dream?*

This was where I drew the line and where my mind started to mess with me.

If I didn't do this, did it mean I would be single forever?

My beliefs were strong, but now I am thinking I was starting to doubt them and myself.

At that point in my life, I had not heard the word "ego" except in the term 'egomaniac'. Again, remember there wasn't social media, or even cell phones besides the big clunky ones. "You've got mail" was about it. Daily Candy was our source of inspiration. Remember Daily Candy anyone? I LOVED the Daily Candy email!

With fear and hesitation, I politely passed on her suggestion. I said prayers to God hoping it wasn't the wrong decision, and I was royally screwing up my chances for love.

I was very torn. The decision not to go through with her direction haunted me. It haunted me for years. Her words rang in my ears, "You will not find love until you clear your past and this is the way to do that."

Whenever a relationship didn't work out, or I was feeling alone, I would revert to that reading. It was painful. What a total mind fuck (excuse my French). But I had to find faith and believe that someone would cross my path without putting $1,000 in my underpants. *Gross, huh?*

I carried this memory with me until that day I got married to Ryan. I wish I knew what I know now back then. It would have saved me a lot of mental anguish and mind loops.

Further, we all have these little voices in our heads that we rarely share with anyone. They can consume us, hurt or destroy our energy, and even pop out in ways that are not kind. We often don't share them because we are ashamed or embarrassed and afraid of judgment. Even bigger than the shame, embarrassment or judgment is when we don't recognize them or acknowledge them.

Imagine if you could become aware, acknowledge and even discuss them so they weren't a "big deal" anymore and you moved past it. You were at peace and felt comfortable talking about what's going on in your head with someone like your spouse/partner or a friend, or even just recognizing them alone to yourself? What would that look like to you? How would you feel?

People have things in their heads that they don't share for those reasons. I intend to share stories that help that little voice realize you are not alone, and you are not crazy.

And finally, layers. I talk about communication layers in CMFC, but there are also thought layers related to spiritual guidance and overcoming your mind. And it often takes time to stop doubting them and unpack them.

In this book, I will also share some insight into thought layers which sometimes involve triggers and energy. It's important to become aware of them, work through them, and move forward. Our guides and all the tools can help with this. They are here for us!

> "What lies behind us and what lies before us are tiny matters compared to what lies within us."
> —Ralph Waldo Emerson

Truth. Let's conquer this inner game and build some confidence.

Chapter 2
The Smoothie

"Go and enjoy your day. Be at peace and know that you have done nothing wrong. Everything is unfolding as it should. Savor your accomplishments and hard earned knowledge and you will find more."
—Akasha Unleashed

(No joke, that quote jumped into my feed…thank you!)

IS IT A SMOOTHIE, MILKSHAKE, green juice, or maybe a mudslide? Wow, a mudslide would be very tasty right now, but then what kind of writing would pop out if I were half in the bag? Probably not a great idea. I will stick to a smoothie.

Sorry, I digress…but you will see my point shortly.

Do you ever stop to think about all the content you consume daily? Or weekly, monthly etc.? Back in "the day," access to all of this knowledge was not at our fingertips.

Sometimes I get nervous and judge myself that the content that pours out of me may be overwhelming, confusing or over the majority of the population's heads. I judge myself harshly, compare myself to others and think of how I can pipe down or streamline.

But I can't seem to do it. Scripting doesn't feel good to me, and I struggle with being more mapped out in content creation; aka "batching," like a lot of social media experts suggest. Batching is when you block a significant amount of time to get a portion of your content done. For example, you may choose to batch two months' worth of podcasts and get them all done in one day. I have tried this, and it doesn't work for me and how I am wired. Thoughts, content, messages come to me as needed, and I present them as such. In other words, I am being guided on what to say when and what feels good.

Hence how I have gotten to a place of thinking my communication can be a smoothie. The energy around a smoothie is more fun and positive than thinking of chopped-up leftovers. As I know this book will be a lot of woven stories, learnings, and circling back to help make a message stick.

I circle back to the fact that I am a Communicator. "A what?" If you know what I mean by saying a Communicator, kudos!

But, many may not, and that's okay. When we all can realize we were not born knowing something, we had to learn it through something or someone; we let go of the judgment we place on ourselves for not knowing. So you can relax if it's your first time hearing that term; I just learned this in the spring of 2020, well into my spiritual journey. Again, no judgment.

Enter my good friend and one of my spiritual teachers, Debbra Lupien. Debbra is an international bestselling author and the Voice of the Akashic Records. With all my heart and soul, I believe that people are meant to be in each other's paths, and when the timing is right it will happen. I met Debbra on my first Zoom call in a mastermind.

She was new to the group, as well. I HAD to talk to her more and have her as a guest on my podcast Good Karma Success Coach. Mind you, I had no clue what the Voice of the Akashic Records meant. I didn't care because I believe in my spirit team and angels. I just knew it was all good stuff.

I became a quick study. Buying Debbra's book, *Akasha Unleashed—The Missing Manual to You*, was the start of the journey. I remember sitting in my backyard in my lawn chair reading the book. It was during Covid-19 when everyone was in lockdown. I was scheduled to be on a sales call where the sales manager would be directing us to start promoting the company on Instagram.

At the time, I was a commission-based sales rep for this company. They were not paying me a salary. Quite the opposite; they were taking 40% of my earned commission. Further, I was fully aware that it wasn't my company and social media should be about your life or building your brand (if you are smart). It had rubbed me the wrong way that this meeting was on my calendar. It did not feel good from any viewpoint and I couldn't shake this awful manipulated feeling.

"When the student is ready, the teacher appears."

I am sure you have heard that saying before. It's been said to be of Theosophical movement, but there are various opinions you can see on Google. Gotta love Google!

Regardless of where the saying derived from, it's true.

One beautiful sunny afternoon during Covid-19 lockdown, I was happily sitting in my lawn chair, trying to forget the chaos and sadness of the outside world. At the same time as sitting with those emotions, my thoughts were heavily burdened with this upcoming meeting on my calendar. I knew in my heart that the meeting would only serve the company's purpose, not mine.

However, as I continued to read Debbra's book, I began to feel a sense of peace wash over me, and it started to click that I needed to choose what felt good and that it was okay to do that. Often, we don't get the approval that it's okay to do what pleases us. People pleasers fall into this category all the time. However, I don't consider myself a people pleaser, which shows you anyone can fall into this mind loop pleasing trap.

Debbra channels Archangel Metatron. Metatron is the keeper of the Akashic Records.

The Akashic Records is a compilation of all universal events, thoughts, words, emotions, intent, ever to have occurred in the past, present or future in terms of all entities and life forms, not just human. (Wikipedia)

Imagine having access to this kind of information to help guide your life?

As I was reading, many sections either in Debbra's words or Metatron's words kept falling in line with the same vibe.

"Ditch the call!" It was like this little garden angel (or maybe fairy, as they are known to be more "naughty") was sitting on my shoulder teaching me a lesson in doing what feels good and trusting my gut that it wasn't going to be a good use of time to be on the Zoom call. If I listened to my lower self, I would have been scared of getting in trouble (*Yes, getting in trouble at age 49—sad, huh?*) and gone on the call, gotten out of alignment, wasted my time, gotten upset/angry at myself, and not been at peace enjoying the lovely day learning and now sharing this story to help others.

See how that works? It's a circle. It's a blended smoothie.

Chapter 3
Spiritual Hobby

"When passion meets work, work becomes a hobby."
—Aniekee Tochukwu Ezekiel

SOMETIMES I FEEL LIKE THIS spiritual, personal development journey is my hobby. I feel inspired to get this off my chest and out of my head in case someone else ever feels this way…you are not alone!

I always struggled with finding a hobby.

I was often reminded that I wasn't a talented child. *Limiting beliefs anyone?*

I attempted many hobbies in my quest to find something I was good at besides work, reading magazines and hanging by the pool. I tried painting, spending countless hours at Michael's craft store. I took a jewelry-making class, the kind where I got to use the torch. I was very impressed that I didn't singe my eyebrows!

I spent a small fortune at a fancy high-end outdoor retailer, REI, in Minneapolis, MN. I bought all the clothes to snowshoe ski and never skied even once. *AND what the heck was I thinking? I hate the cold!*

I bought every workout DVD and coordinating equipment you can imagine. I even once bought a hula hoop! *Yep. Waste.*

Then in November 2005, I wrote down that for a husband, I wanted a dark curly-haired guy with a big smile who was taller than me and had a hobby. Yes, I asked the Universe to bring me a guy with a hobby. I had no clue what I was doing, but had heard about making a list. So, why not, right? And the Universe delivered.

My husband is an "obsessed" charter boat fishing guide captain. Talk about an expensive hobby!

Initially, it was super fun! Weekends on the river or a lake, I would bring my magazines and chair and he would fish for hours on the bank. We would have lunch somewhere and it was an adventure.

Now, the hobby is his job. Well, actually, a business. Albeit, a business we are both very proud of so don't get me wrong, I am not complaining, BUT be careful what you wish for!

The point of my story is that in the traditional sense, I am still hobby-less. In my craziness of desiring a guy who looked like he stepped off a steamy romance novel cover but had a hobby, too, I still didn't find my own hobby.

I guess I thought that whatever he liked to do, I would like to do, too. And if I had a quarter for every time someone asked me, "Melinda, do you go fishing with Ryan?" I would be rich!

The answer is, "No, maybe two times a year. He fishes. I eat Fritos, dance around, and pray I don't get seasick." *Seriously.*

So, where am I now? I finally found my hobby: spiritual discovery.

Books, audio, podcasts, oracle and tarot decks, crystals, pendulums, energy rods, white candles, and many courses later, I can comfortably say that my spiritual development journey is a working hobby. Oh! And let's not forget the readings! Surely I am forgetting something else, too.

But, here's the thing, hobbies are fun, and we love them! Otherwise, like the fishing was for me, we don't do them. So, looking at spiritual development as a working hobby is way more fun and positive way of looking at it than thinking of it as a job. Or in my case, as a coach and author, it's the best of both worlds!

> "Hobbies just sort of gradually become my vocation."
> —Weird Al Yankovic

And to boot, isn't it fun when you buy something and feel good and know it contributes to your overall growth? It's such a win-win!

So, I challenge anyone who may be struggling with, "Do I need another tarot deck?" "Should I purchase this book on manifestation when I have 50 manifestation books already on my shelves?" "Should I sit on this Zoom meditation call, too?" Permit yourself to do what makes your heart sing with joy, and you will get a little wiser, confident, and abundant with each step.

If you can use it in your business, like I do, and help others, all the better!

> "Doing what you love is the cornerstone of having abundance in your life."
> —Dr. Wayne Dyer

Chapter 4
Discovering Kabbalah

> "It may surprise you to learn that a positive outcome to this journey is guaranteed."
> —Michael Berg

IF YOU CANNOT TELL BY now, I have a very curious side to me.

My sister, Debra, would say that I am nosy.

I would say that she is jealous. *I love my sister!*

Curiosity has served me well, and I am proud of this trait. It has led me to all of these amazing tools, teachers, and learnings which I am now sharing to help you on your journey.

I met my good friend Terry DeMonaco in October, 2010. We met at a trade show, as we were both sales reps at the time. I struggled with meeting friends and didn't fit into The Florida Keys vibe, so when I met Terry, I was so happy!

Terry gets full credit for introducing me to Kabbalah. I was raised attending a Presbyterian church and never felt connected to religion. I had a very tough time with judgment, as I could feel it even as a young girl. It was odd to be looked at as if I wasn't wealthy enough to attend our church.

The church we attended was in a nice area of a south suburb of Chicago. In Bible classes, I felt the other kids looked down their noses at me because I didn't live in their town. We lived in the next town over. It was an odd feeling to have at such a young age. I didn't connect with anyone. My mom made us go to Confirmation class, Wednesday night Bible study, and we attended Sunday services about 50% of the time.

The best thing about the Wednesday night Bible study was that we ate mac-n-cheese with ham for dinner. Seriously.

Attending Sunday service varied depending on my parents' weekend plans. When we didn't "have to go" to church, I felt this massive sense of relief. I wanted to be connected to God and learn about Jesus, but not in that way. It felt forced and uncomfortable. At that age, I could never explain it and I certainly didn't talk about it. But, the feeling was there.

I also had this fear of the Bible. I had put cute fun colorful stickers on the inside cover. I did it with love! I loved stickers; I collected them and they made me happy. In my mind, I wasn't defacing anything, I was decorating it with love. But when my mom saw the stickers in the Bible, oh, she was mad! I can still feel it to this day. I then became ashamed to carry my Bible, and I would place my hand over the cover where it was ripped to hide it so the pastor wouldn't see it and yell at me.

During Bible study, it consumed my mind, so I couldn't even focus on the lesson. I don't know why I ever thought he would yell at me; he never yelled at anyone. He was very kind, and I liked him. But the fear was there. I still have the Bible, and you can still see where the stickers were. And yep, this many years later it still brings up some anxiety.

> "We cannot escape the results of past actions, but we
> may change the results by what we do now."
> —Rav Berg

As I have gotten older, I have learned more about the church, how it originated, and how it is a business whether you want to admit it or not. I am not saying anything is wrong with religion or church, but it wasn't for me. I like and respect business. But I felt at peace when I finally realized the differences and let it go. If you read CMFC, you read the story about me even trying church again in my 20's to meet a boyfriend. I hope you liked that story. It's a doozy!

When Terry introduced me to Kabbalah, I had to say this was the first spiritual practice that inspired me. Prior to Kabbalah, I was operating on my intuition sprinkled with some Joel Osteen. Yes, he is a church preacher, but I focused on the positive messages and felt sharing Joel's messages with Ryan helped him, as well.

When I met Kabbalah, it spoke to me and helped me to connect the dots of my life as I learned more and more about it. I became a sponge. I wore the red string for about a year and absorbed every piece of information I could find. Books, books on CD, and anything Terry felt like sharing with me.

The Red String Bracelet

Are you familiar with the meaning of the red string bracelet? Most people associate Kabbalah with the red string, but other religions also wear it, including Christianity, Buddhism, and Hinduism.

It is said to have true fortune, you must be protected from the negative energy of others.

The red string, worn on the left wrist, wards off misfortune and dark energies said to be brought on by the evil eye. The left side is the receiving side of the body and soul, and the red string should be knotted seven times, as around Rachel's Tomb. The color red signifies courage, bravery and reminds us of our tongue and the importance of compassion to others. The red string is mentioned in the Bible in Genesis 38.

It is important that you have someone you love and trust tie the red string around your wrist and knot it seven times.

In addition, below is the Ben Porat Prayer, which should also be recited as someone is tying the knot.

> *"Ayin alei porat ben Yosef porat benyivarech ra mikol oti hagoel hamalachshmi bahem vyikare han'arim etvYitzchak Avraham avotai vshemha'aretz b'kerev larov v'yidgu."*

Do your best with the prayer. It's most important to be in a positive energy state and say positive affirmations while implementing this. If you are not feeling positive, please wait and do it another time.

The bracelet will eventually wear out and fall off. It is said to have absorbed enough bad energy, and when you feel ready, you can replace it following the same guidance.

The Kabbalah Center

Terry lived in southeast Florida at the time, near a Kabbalah center in Boca Raton. She could easily go to services and events whereas for me, living in The Florida Keys, it was not as feasible. I was able to attend one meeting on Astrology, for which I was grateful. I loved the overall message and felt it kick-started my journey into taking ownership of my behavior, understanding where it stemmed from, and working toward becoming a better person.

I often feel like religious institutions aim to separate themselves from others. Do you agree? I know this stems from history, but there are so many good things about a lot of religions. To me, Kabbalah had a bridge-like sparkly vibe. Simply put, it's about living your best life, relationships, astrology, prosperity, and more. It didn't matter that I wasn't Jewish, Kabbalah was accepting. My friend Terry wasn't Jewish and to my observation, there wasn't any separation or judgment.

Kabbalah helped increase my knowledge and understanding of:

- Ego and the different ways ego creeps up and affects your life.
- The energetics of money.
- Our garbage is our gift and the concept of personal correction.

In general, Kabbalah helped me connect the dots and realize there was more out there than attending traditional church, as I had grown up. It was eye-opening. There was a lot for me to learn and much work to be done.

The journey into extreme personal development was just beginning. This chapter is just a nugget. If you are interested in learning more about Kabbalah, I would suggest the book, *Living Kabbalah—A Practical System for Making the Power Work for You* by Yehuda Berg.

> "The moment you accept your being, who you are, is the flow of Light, and the moment you tune into that flow, everything around you will be illuminated."
> —Karen Berg

Chapter 5

The Tarot Card Reading that Changed Everything

"Jesus Take the Wheel."
—Carrie Underwood

NOT MANY PEOPLE KNOW THIS story. Why is that? Oh goodness…so many reasons…*where do I start?*

If you read *Confidence Mastery for Couples (CMFC)*, I share a bit about being single for a long time (eons! in my opinion) and then finally meeting my husband, Ryan. There is a whole relationship section that I left out and saved for this book. It's a crazy juicy tale, and depending on your beliefs, a kind of unbelievable one.

In my early thirties, I met a guy named Scott while I lived in Columbus, Ohio.

As mentioned in CMFC, I desperately wanted a boyfriend. Along came Scott. I believe the best in people; innately we all do, hence why toxic relationships, domestic violence, scams, etc. exist. We all want the best for ourselves and for others, so often our judgment gets clouded. My own judgment was in that cloudy stormy bucket at that time.

Once in a while, a little ray of sunlight (clarity) would pop out, and then for some reason my "desperate to have a boyfriend brain" would ignore it and the thick clouds would cover it up. Scott was a toxic liar. Over the years, besides a little white lie here and there that was stupid and virtually harmless, I had never known someone to lie.

We met while he was still in college. I was about 31 years old, and he was only a few years younger than me. It struck me as odd that he was still in college. Scott told me that he had played basketball in Europe for years, so that was why he was behind in getting his degree.

Scott had begged when we met, "Please don't ever talk to my parents about me playing basketball in Europe, because they were never happy with my decision and I don't want to stir up any bad conversations."

I thought it seemed like a logical request. Parents can get upset over odd things, so I didn't think much of the request. He was tall and good at basketball from what I could tell, so I rolled with it. During our time together, I had come to realize his parents were amazing people and extremely supportive of their son.

Prior to us meeting, he had attended two different colleges. At the time of our meeting, he was at his third college. Since people transfer schools, some starting at a local or junior college, it didn't register to be anything but normal. But then, all of the sudden, he had to transfer to another college, Ohio State University. I thought this was odd, but again my faith and trust brought back the clouds to cover that ray of sunshine. This was his 4th college…hmm…

Then, as many couples do regardless of how toxic the situation is, we got engaged. I was finally getting married and over the moon excited. I worked obsessively to plan my dream wedding on the beach in Hilton Head, SC. The wedding was set for June the following year, making our engagement about a year and a half.

During the time in which we were engaged, I had moved to Dayton, Ohio to be closer to my retail buying job with Elder Beerman Department Stores. I had been in a horrific car accident on my commute from Columbus to Dayton which spurred my desire to move. I was en route to work on an elevated two-lane interstate when across the ravine I saw a truck with chickens had been in an accident.

It was nuts! Chickens were flying everywhere. I noticed the chaos and slowed down along with the cars in front of me and to my right. However, a big green semi behind me didn't notice the slowdown and was still traveling over 70 miles an hour.

Talk about "Jesus Take the Wheel" in action. I have chills recounting the memory right now. It was beyond awful. I was boxed in traffic and had to absorb the hit. I didn't have an option. To my left was the cement wall and in the middle between the other two lanes of traffic was the ravine. To my right a line of cars and in front of me a solid pack of cars. It was the typical morning commute into Dayton.

I sat, prayed, "Dear God help me," gripped the wheel, and watched in my rearview mirror as he got closer and closer until he pummeled into me from behind.

It was amazing that I survived with only some minor damage to my teeth. It wasn't my day to die and that was clear. But my car was totaled, and the event led me to have panic attacks while driving whenever I would see a green semi-truck.

Suddenly, a few months later, Scott told me he was transferring to the college in Dayton. They supposedly had a better education program, and we could live together.

Now, I was starting to get upset. I never had a clear understanding of how many credits he had, how much debt in student loans, and when the heck he was going to graduate! People would ask me all the time, "When is Scott going to graduate?" Embarrassing, as I didn't know how to answer. Here I was, a four-year college graduate from Purdue University with an excellent career and I didn't know when my fiancé would graduate? Geez, a lot of shame was starting to build.

I considered myself to be a smart woman. To add to the shame and embarrassment, I started to get concerned as I was primarily the one paying for everything. He couldn't seem to hold a job, and wasn't moving forward towards a career and stability. Now he was moving in with me, which meant I was paying for rent, groceries, utilities, etc. During our time living together, there were bouts of drunken behavior when he would lock himself in the spare bedroom and tell me he was "pretend gambling online."

One day, I remember he wouldn't get out of bed and he had a final exam to take. I couldn't stop thinking about the situation and it was consuming my morning. I lied to my boss and said my iron was still on and I had to go home to turn it off. I quickly left the office, during a major snowstorm, to get him out of bed and to his exam. Seriously.

That I was in my thirties and dealing with this situation was above and beyond ridiculous. Was I a babysitter or a fiancé? If someone really suffered from depression or something was wrong, I would understand. But his intention was from another realm of being enabled and toxicity. I felt like I was losing my sanity. An out of control spinning that I didn't know how to fix and was too embarrassed to talk about.

A surprise twist happened a few months after Scott moved in. Elder Beerman was purchased by another retailer (Bon Ton), and even though the company said they would keep the offices in Dayton, I knew in my gut that the offices would be closing. I already had my resume together, as I was unhappy at work, and was in the process of interviewing with Target in Minneapolis, MN. In July of the same year we got engaged, I moved to Minneapolis to start working for Target. According to Scott, he only had a little over a year left, so the plan was for me to move and get settled and then he would follow me to Minnesota after graduation; a plan that appeared to be solid. I was super excited about my new job and moving to Minneapolis.

That summer we went to visit my friends, Karen and Christopher, in The Hamptons for a long weekend. They were friends from when I lived in NYC. My friends happen to be very well-traveled, which I am not. Karen started asking Scott questions about his time in Europe and what sites he saw. A few times, I could see her make a confused face about him not knowing what European landmarks she was referring to and confusion about the fact he said he didn't visit any of the landmarks. From her experience, they were popular sites so she wondered why he wouldn't have visited them. Karen and I never talked about it further. But the conversations stuck with me and started to repeat in my brain. They were major red flags, but I kept going as I was excited to get married.

The winter before we were to be married, Scott called suddenly wanting to transfer his car to my name and get MN plates. The way he explained it made sense since he was moving to MN (someday, right?), and his license plate tags were up for renewal.

He was going to fly up to MN to visit me, bring the car title, and we could get the tags changed over. *"Sure, sounds good," I said, "Why not get more ready for the move?"* He had this grand master plan, but I still never could get a clear answer on his graduation and neither could his parents. The responses were always grey.

The months went by, and I was very happy planning the wedding and learning about my new buying job with Target, until the phone call came.

My phone rang late at night, and it was a police officer in Ohio.
"Is this Melinda Anderson?"
"Yes."
"Do you own a 20XX Toyota in Ohio?"
"Yes."

At this moment, still trying to wake, I was so confused about what was going on. The last late-night surprise phone call I had received was just a few months earlier when my parents called me to tell me my brother, Bryan, had tragically passed away. It was too soon to get another call like that. My heart was pounding as I was trying to get my wits about me.

The officer proceeded to tell me that Scott was illegally driving "my car." Scott's driver's license was suspended for drunk driving, and therefore, he was under arrest for driving without a license.

Wow. Are you kidding me? Or is this a hidden camera show? I thought.

Not only was his license suspended for drunk driving, which in my opinion as well as millions of other people's opinion is a major deal, but then the car now in my name was a complete lie. *What else had he lied about?*

The clouds opened up and all the situations, excuses, covering up started to click. I couldn't believe how all of the sudden ALL these memories and conversations came rushing to me.

- The school situation
- The trip to The Hamptons
- Locking himself in the spare bedroom
- Lying about classes and exams, jobs

Just to name a few…

It was all a lie. And we were two weeks away from the wedding. I was above and beyond confused and didn't know what to do.

Was I in the Twilight Zone?

I was completely freaked out.

My heart beats on forgiveness. I had plans to see my family that weekend. It was not going to be the first time I would have to share some not-so-great update about Scott with my parents. I was petrified. My father was paying for the wedding in Hilton Head. It was going to take place at one of the most excellent beach resorts on the island, Palmetto Dunes. There were over 70 people committed to attending and everyone was excited and looking forward to the occasion.

A gorgeous ocean blue chocolate seashell-designed cake (I love cake), my perfect pink silk custom dress I designed with gorgeous pink satin gem-stone high heels I searched high and low for, even an ice sculpture; every detail was perfectly planned. All the things a girl dreams of! PLUS, wasn't I in love?

The confusion on how to handle this was tragic. I had not spoken to Scott as it was too much stress. So, I put him on pause to head to Illinois and see what my family thought. After bawling my eyes out until there were no tears left, my parents were surprisingly calm. The end result was left up to me:

1. We could tell everyone the wedding was off, but everyone could still come and have a party since it was already paid for.

Or

2. We could proceed as planned.

Again, my heart beats on forgiveness. *How could someone not learn from this and never ever make a mistake like this again?*
Angels Do Exist. (Chills)
Wow, it was tough, but I still had some vision of optimism. So, I tried to forgive him and we had the wedding as planned.

I drove us to and from the wedding, hoping none of our friends would question why I was always driving. I sucked up my extreme embarrassment and shame.

I flew first to Ohio from Minnesota, then took a cab to his apartment and picked him up in the car, which was now in my name, and drove to Hilton Head; all while dealing with mind loops, anger, resentment, and fear. I was furious, but the show was on and I had to find a way to push through the feelings.

The wedding itself and the week following was an absolute blast! It would be unfair to ever say anything less. We all got along, had fun and it worked out beautifully. It was sad that my brother wasn't with us, but since that day I have lost my very good friend from college, Amy, my brother-in-law Jason, and both of my grandparents, so I will always treasure that event and the memories of those who attended.

But after the wedding, Scott and I were alone again. We went on our honeymoon, which was a short cruise leaving out of Florida. He was drunk the entire time, and it was a stressful disaster. I was desperately trying to find out if he would ever graduate and we could move forward.

Me, "Hey Scott, when do you think you will graduate?"
Scott, "Not sure."
Me, "How many credits do you have?"
Scott, "Need to check."
Same story, different day.
No conclusion.

After the cruise, I drove back up to Ohio, handed the car over to his wonderful, kind parents and flew back to Minnesota.

I tried to get back to normal. August was the next time we had planned to see each other. Two months after the wedding, Scott flew up to Minneapolis and we were sitting on the floor watching television when I vividly remember receiving a phone call from his uncle from Maine who had been our wedding officiant.

"Melinda and Scott, I have something to tell you. You are not really married."

What? What's he talking about? We went to the courthouse in Beaufort and got our marriage license, we did all the things. I mailed the signed license to the state. What's going on?

It turned out that his uncle was not registered and certified in the state of South Carolina, which was a requirement that none of us had realized existed. And then it dawned on me that the previous day I had received a letter from Beaufort County, South Carolina, and I hadn't opened it yet. I ran and got the letter, and it said the same thing: "You are not married."

Wow. I sat in silence, stunned. It was a super odd feeling; a ginormous mixed bag of "WTF mush."

Then "The Brilliant Scott" (that's how I felt when he said this) said to me, "Well, that's a good thing for you probably because you would be responsible for my student loans, and I would not be able to get them anymore with your salary."

Are you f-ing kidding me? Now you tell me this. Am I in another galaxy? For real?

The weekend ended with a big thud. After that, it was a blur of lies on my end and of course, another super fun discussion with my family. We decided to keep it secret (yep, now I am a liar) and only tell my sister, her husband, and my grandparents. The plan became to then go to the courthouse in Minnesota when he finally graduated and get legally married. When would he graduate was still the million dollar question. But, that was the plan.

I was so confused by all the drama. I had been through so much; my brother dying the prior December, extreme job stress, and now this: a long distance, non-trustworthy lie of a marriage. Something had to give. So, during that time, I rarely saw or spoke to Scott. It was on pause as much as possible so I could continue to figure my shit out. I was at the end of my rope on what I could handle. Exhausted.

The next time I remember seeing him was in June for our "anniversary." Ha! I flew to Dayton for the weekend. Scott had his driver's license back by then, and he was living in some teeny tiny apartment that had barely anything. I remember going to the local Meijer store, and he parked in a parking spot for the handicap. That blew my mind. I lost it, as I could never take advantage of something that is meant for someone who has a challenge.

Scott and I were both blessed to be able to walk. I strongly felt and still feel that it would be bad karma to take advantage and do something so dishonest.

So parking the car in this parking spot continued to show what kind of person he was. I went into the store and when I came out, he was gone. He literally left me at the Meijer.

Yep, left me. Nice huh? *Happy Fucking Anniversary to me.*

Luckily, his apartment was only a few blocks away. I walked to his apartment. After screaming and yelling, which didn't result in any remorse or apology, I flew back to Minnesota the next day. Even after I left, he never apologized.

My rope had turned into a thread and the increasing stress at work made me put the situation on the back burner again. We weren't married, he lived in Ohio, and I could ignore it some more while I dealt with my work stress. Both aspects were painful because I knew if I lost my job, I didn't have a husband's salary to fall back on.

A few weeks after, I got another call from the police.

Again, he was in jail for driving drunk without a license. This time it was his parents' vehicle and they received the call, as well. It was time to face the truth and have a chat with his parents.

I had come to love his parents. As I had mentioned earlier, they were kind, loving people. I really really liked them a lot. I often struggled with wondering if I loved his parents more than him, as I had always craved a larger, fun family. Mine just kind of sat around at the holidays, but his family was fun. So, having the conversation with his parents was more challenging than expected.

They were disappointed. We talked about all the lies, and they were as kind as could be.

They said, "If I was their daughter, they would advise me to walk away."

I needed to sit with this. *Did I love him? Would he ever change?*

I was confused not only about whether I loved him or not but also if could I forgive him. I felt like the biggest fool. Embarrassment and shame were no longer strong enough words to hide my emotions and my health was starting to deteriorate. I don't suffer from anxiety, but anxiety appeared like an unwelcome friend. It was eating at me in the form of weight loss and exhaustion. On top of that, I was living the lie that we were married.

Again, I needed to tell my parents, who I am pretty sure were above and beyond over this whole chaotic scenario. I couldn't blame them; the nightmare was not ending.

My mom was into tarot card readings as much as I was. I remember this so clearly. We were hanging in the pool at my parents' house in IL. I loved that pool! It was a big pool, without trees, so all bright sunshine, and it was peaceful. We seemed to have the majority of our discussions in the pool.

So, hanging in the pool, she proceeds to tell me a story.

Before the wedding, she had decided to get her tarot cards read. She was concerned about the marriage, as well.

The tarot card reader told her, "Not to worry about the wedding, your son, Bryan (my brother who had passed away), would take care of it."

Giving you some time to let that soak in…I still often am wowed.

He did. Bryan sure took care of it. He worked in conjunction with the Universe so it aligned that we didn't actually get married. Amazing how things all work out as they should.

My brother, Bryan, who I miss with all my heart, was watching out for me and took care of it.

Thank you, Bryan!

Who do you know that has a wedding that, unintentionally, isn't a wedding?

My mom had "let it go." Her mind had been put at ease with the reading from that day.

And sure enough, it came to pass. It worked out as God had planned, for us to just have a big party.

Now, it was time to figure out what the heck to finally do.

The Renaissance Festival

I had been ignoring the issue, and it was time to move forward. The Universe knew it was time to move on, as this part is incredible.

Outside of Minneapolis, every fall, was a very popular Renaissance festival. I had been DYING to go. I love fairies and all things magical, and this festival was set up like an authentic village and was there for about six weeks. I had heard fabulous things but I had never been. Several of my cooking club girlfriends and I decided to attend. Of course, there were tarot card and fortune teller readers. What would a festival be without magical readers?

Upon arriving, my eyes, ears, and nose couldn't take in all of the excitement fast enough. Food, drinks, shopping, and people all dressed up in character. HUGE Turkey legs and beer to drink out of big mugs. So fun! The festival was on point with the feel of being in that period. Best yet, I was entranced by the beautiful ladies dressed up as sparkly fairies and was extremely envious as they pranced around talking magical talk. *If only...*

We all signed up for a half-hour reading. None of us knew any of the readers and you signed up on a general list, so even if I did know one of the readers, you were assigned a reader by chance or fate.

I intuitively chose to take my ring off. I don't know why.

Maybe in my heart, I knew this horrible sham of a marriage was over?

Maybe I wanted to see what she would have to say and not have any clues?

Here is where it gets bizarre...

I can't make this up...

It was my turn to go into the tent for a reading. The reader, Elizabeth, seemed very friendly and kind. She was maybe in her fifties and just seemed like a very normal lady.

As in typical fashion, she asked me if I had any questions, what did I want to talk about. She shuffled the cards. I left it open, closed my eyes, and took a deep breath.

Are you ready for this?

The first thing out of her mouth was, "You are married but not married. And he will never change. You need to move on."

I will give you a moment to take it in. *I still need a moment when I recount it.*

The rest of the reading was pretty much a blur except for more information about Scott and how he would never change no matter how hard I worked on the relationship.

I was stunned.

And since none of my friends knew that I wasn't really married I couldn't share the story. I had to keep this revelation and guidance inside and end this relationship ASAP.

It was final. It was done. I confidently made the phone call to end the broken relationship, paid him an agreed upon amount for the wedding gifts, and moved on. We never spoke again.

Never.

Thank you, Elizabeth!

Not the end of my readings with Elizabeth

I barely had time to fill people in on why I wasn't married anymore when I went on match.com and met Ryan. It all happened so fast.

At this time in my life, I didn't know a thing about energy; had never even heard the word "energy" mentioned outside of the typical way an average human thinks of energy: light bulbs, electrical sockets, microwaves, and curling irons, to name a few.

However, I knew it didn't feel good to recount the story time and time again to everyone.

I trusted my gut in that. Ryan and I met on December 16, 2005, three months after I officially ended things with Scott.

We got engaged on February 14, 2006. *Yep that fast.* The majority of people were confused, as they thought I was already married. It was definitely a bit uncomfortable to explain.

If you have read CMFC, you know that I am very transparent that my marriage with Ryan has not always been sunshine and rainbows, and we always are doing the work. So, in light of that transparency, to say we had a rocky start is an understatement.

I needed help. Here I was on the same path of managing drinking, poor behavior, my control issues, and high expectations. It was a very similar cycle but just different dynamics, situations, and circumstances.

I was confused, depressed, and angry at the relationship I had gotten myself into again.

Thank goodness I keep business cards!

I scheduled the call.

Elizabeth did not remember me.

I loved that! I had a fresh start, a clean slate. I was anxious to hear what she had to say.

Wow, as I sit here remembering this, I often mention rainbows and that is what she said:

"It is tough, but he will get better."

"You are meant to be together, and at the end, it will be a rainbow."

That sealed it and gave me the peace and confidence that everything with Ryan would be okay.

Even though I have always held strong faith and belief in tarot card readings, I am sure there are doubters. For me, it's like having a trusted friend or therapist who can guide you along with the Universe. Nothing better than that. I don't think I have ever had a friend who I recommended to a reader be disappointed.

If you are someone who is new to tarot and wishes to use the spiritual tool for guidance I would recommend listening to The Good Karma Success Coach Podcast Episode 104 Conversation with Deb Frueh. "What Can You Learn From Tarot?"

Another tool is Joanna Hunter's, Intuitive Tarot online course. I have taken it and love it! Even if you are not aiming to be a reader, the online course helps to learn more about tarot cards and intuition. Joanna was a guest on The Good Karma Success Coach Podcast as well, Episode 100. "Manifesting Secrets."

And check out the show notes for both podcasts to connect with these amazing teachers.

Building a spiritual toolbox and using gifts, such as tarot, along with your intuition, will help guide you even on your darkest days. But, you need to take inspired action and start the process.

> "No one saves us from ourselves. No one can and no one may. We ourselves must walk the path."
> —Buddha

Chapter 6

Bread Crumbs

> "This is the sign you have been looking for."
> —Unknown

9:30 A.M. EST, APRIL 15, 2021—"Stephanie, did you get paid this month?"

At the time of writing this chapter, I have represented a vendor for 11 years. Now it is a side hustle and a fun way to earn some extra cash. I discovered this vendor walking the aisles at a NYC Accessory Trade Show when I was the buyer for a television shopping network.

I remember the day I showed the vendor to upper management. My memory of that day is so clear. My direct boss, Debbie, hated the products; she thought they were the ugliest things she had ever seen. My VP, Karen, didn't like them either, however, she trusted my judgment. She allowed me to have one hour of airtime to what we called "test the concept." As a buyer, it was a huge win for the vendor and for me. I was proud to have the opportunity and had confidence they would be a hit with our customers.

I was right.

The product sold out in 10 minutes. It was crazy! It was wild! I remember watching on the TV in my office freaking out with excitement! The owner had never been on live TV before so he didn't even realize what was going on. The whole team was cheering and then celebrating. And then we had a crazy fast scramble to fill the rest of the hour with product to sell because it was live shopping TV so you couldn't just stop.

A Bread Crumb

When we moved to The Florida Keys in October of 2009, I had started working for a privately held manufacturer who was based in Hong Kong. I was so excited about this position. I had finally found a sales position, and it seemed like the perfect fit. The hard part initially was that there was not an existing account base. None. No one had heard of the company and there wasn't any product to sell. It was all product development. The owner Bruce told me, "They could make anything!" and so I set out on a cold calling war path.

I emailed and networked with everyone I knew. I was 100%+ focused and dedicated. I was going to be a millionaire with this position! There was no doubt in my mind. Not only was LinkedIn my new best friend, but also Alibaba was in its initial stages, and since I was a previous buyer I knew about trade shows.

It was a slow start, *drip* to put it mildly, with so many painful twists and turns. The pain was all the factory and product-based challenges that continued to happen and were out of my control. Not to mention the fact that my boss had a Jekyll and Hyde personality. One second he was a like big brother and so kind and funny, the next he was a demon screaming at me. I share a story in CMFC about him, as well.

In May of 2010, I had a breaking point with the manufacturer. It wasn't the final straw, but it was a rough patch. The first apartment

Ryan and I lived at in The Florida Keys had a nice quiet private beach. I remember going out to the beach and sobbing about something that went wrong that I was not able to fix. It was another notch in a very beat up board (me) and I was exhausted.

I sat on the beach sobbing like a wild maniac and praying for help. Luckily, no one was around that day. The little beach was normally overrun with Air BNB vacationers, so my angels were definitely looking out for me to have this time in quiet.

A few hours later, after I calmed myself down, I was flipping through a magazine. It was either *Elle* or *Bazaar*, I cannot remember which. But I had seen an advertisement for the vendor's products. It was very pretty and that magazine ad ended up being a breadcrumb. I emailed the owner and the sales manager to say hello and compliment the ad. I didn't have any intention except to say hello and compliment the ad.

I heard back immediately both the owner and the sales manager asking, "Where are you? What are you doing?"

I briefly explained where we were living and that I was building a business as a sales rep. Again, it was an innocent hello.

After a catch-up call, they presented me an opportunity to be the road rep for the southern half of Florida. I had never thought about being a road rep before. I knew they existed, but I had always been in the corporate world, so I didn't pay much attention to the smaller boutiques nor did I realize that a road rep is the person who works with the boutiques.

We started with the smaller territory so we could see if the sales position was a fit. I realized I liked it; it was fun meeting the boutique owners and traveling. My new boss eventually gave me the southeastern part of the US. The southeast was comprised of eight states. I quickly learned that was too much territory to do the best job for the company and customers, and not enough ROI for me.

Hmm…how could I make this type of sales business work for me and be profitable?

After giving it some time, I put it out there to the Universe that something needed to change. My desire was to have more vendors and products to sell closer to home to make a prosperous living being a road rep.

Within a short period of time, I was working with a customer in Key West who mentioned a multi-vendor rep group that "couldn't seem to keep a rep." Since I was a buyer and had been to all of the major trade shows, I understood what a multi-vendor rep company was.

I wasn't fully keen on the idea, as they take a cut of the vendor commission as a middle-man, and the rep is the one doing the majority of the work. As with anything there are pluses and minuses, so with some parameters in agreement with the rep group I ventured forward.

Somehow, my sales bread crumbs via the Universe were leading me in a positive direction. Magical!

Within a few years, after a lot of hard work, relationship building and following the crumbs, I had built a sales business from $100K to $2.5M annually.

I lived in my happy money—making bubble for five years. Most companies left me alone and I did my thing. Isn't that nice when you are left alone like a grown up and can work your business and make money for yourself and others? A lot of that has to do with great leadership, which unfortunately changed in 2017.

In March of 2017, the large rep group decided to cut my territory in half. I won't say I manifested this; however I was aware that it could someday happen. Losing half my business that I worked so hard to build was extremely painful. Not only financially, but the rhythm I had going would change. I viewed my business like my baby that I was now having to give up after feeding and nurturing it for five years.

I wrote on a piece of paper from my favorite "I want to be like Barbie, that bitch has everything" notepad, "What is Next? 3-17-17." I still have it on my bulletin board.

What happened in that next year? I started the path to become a success coach after a personal self-discovery journey to see how I could best serve and how I could use the skills I had acquired along with all the lessons and pain to help others. It led me to where I am now.

Late fall of 2018, I took online and virtual coaching classes and became a certified coach with World Coaching Institute (WCI).

Even though I was excited, I played small hiding behind my sales job. I was still making good money as a sales rep and I was afraid of getting fired. A lot of people do this with their side hustles.

It's amazing how money will mess with you. Money can keep you tied to toxic people and poor treatment. So many people live in fear of lack of money. You would think I would have learned this as many times as I have lost jobs or changed jobs but always ended up okay. I still had money fear. I liked having money and didn't want to give it up.

No, let's back that up. I LOVE having money! It was fun to go on vacation, be generous, or buy whatever we needed or desired. I also liked being able to absorb household costs so my husband could put more money into his growing fishing charter business, Good Karma Sportfishing.

I didn't want to go back to that scary place in 2009, when we had nothing. The memories were still too fresh. I just wasn't ready to relive that and give up what I had worked so hard to build. I needed to recoup the loss financially but also mentally.

I dabbled in my new coaching business. April 2018 was the official launch, and I was excited, but still hiding. After a few pro-bono clients that required a lot of time and never took the actions I recommended, I decided that working on becoming a speaker for B2B (business to business) would build income faster, and I could then comfortably quit my sales job.

My memory goes back to 2008 into 2009, when I was thinking I would get a buying job in the South, the company would move us, pay for everything and we would be set!

My guides laugh at my best laid plans…they obviously have their own and fail to tell me what they are.

Nice huh?

Love you, guides!

Leaving it Up to God

In the fall of 2018, I knew the days were becoming numbered on my minivan. My minivan was a gift from God when I needed it.

I had started repping using an old black Jaguar. *Circa...who the heck knows, it was super old!*

The trunk was deep enough to fit several dead bodies—no joke. I swear it was an old Mafia car. So, starting out I could layer in so many suitcases in the trunk as well as the back seat. It was deep and extremely helpful.

Not too far into my road repping journey, the Jaguar started to break down. I would leave for a trip and pray the entire time, "Please God let me get where I need to go safely." Every time.

Then finally, it had a major breakdown outside of Orlando, FL. I think God was tired of hearing me pray daily and having to deal with the car and my journey.

In the middle of a very full agenda, five hours north of my house in The Keys, my old black mafia Jaguar broke down. Luckily, I had AAA Roadside Insurance and could get help. The local Orlando area mechanic didn't have the car part, and the part would not be arriving until the next day. I needed a rental car to get me through the night and be able to see my customers the next day.

What did they have left to borrow? A minivan. Yep, an uncool minivan. It was especially uncool if you are not a mom, parent or and have kids to tow. But heck, I was so grateful to have something that I could fit all my samples and catalogs in and not have to cancel a full day of appointments to hang out in a cheap, drab hotel room.

What ended up happening? I fell in love with the minivan. All joking aside, a minivan is an organized person's, in my case an Aries, generator's, dream machine! It's super spacious, the doors open so easily, and you can pretty much set up an office inside. It was a gift from the Universe! My terrible stressful ordeal the day before and the yuckiness I felt when I saw it melted away when I saw dollar signs of how I work and travel more efficiently. And gosh, do I l LOVE being efficient.

After I returned home with my Jaguar all fixed, at least for the moment, I knew I would have to make a decision. But, since I was still new building my business, our bank account was at zero. Yep, zero. I barely made enough each month to cover our expenses. And Ryan was still starting as well. His client list was small and we were having to buy equipment to outfit the boat as well as pay for advertising to get charters.

The next week I was up north in Deerfield, FL, staying at a lovely (kidding) La Quinta. As I was sitting on the bed watching the TV, a Toyota commercial came on for Kendall Toyota. Kendall is the suburban section of Miami. The minivan that I had set my sights on for the past week was a Toyota Sienna. I also loved the name because Sienna is my oldest niece's name and I had suggested that name to my sister. It was a match! The commercial was about zero money down…yep… the wheels started turning (pun intended).

I came home and told Ryan. He stared at me in his usual fashion. Ryan's stare without a no is always a yes. I took that yes and ran with it. We went that Saturday to Kendall Toyota.

My prayers were consistent…Please God let me be able to buy this car. Again, we had no money, I knew I wasn't going to get anything for the mafia car and who knows how they would look at my average credit score. It wasn't terrible, as I always managed to pay our bills, but it wasn't stellar either. It was a nail biter as we sat there and waited and waited and waited. If you have bought a car before, you know; the process can be quite drawn out. Why? I have no idea, but it's maddening. It's gotten a bit better in the recent years with online car competition, but in 2012, a lot of car transactions were still at the dealer.

Lo and behold, I was approved! And from that day forward, my minivan was God's minivan.

So when the day came in 2018 to acknowledge that the minivan might have been getting close to retirement, it started to eat at my subconscious. *What would I do? What would I buy?* I wasn't feeling drawn to another minivan, but if I didn't have a minivan anymore, did that mean I was not going to be a sales rep? How would I replace that income? Would we be okay?

Wow, I had a lot of energy wrapped up in the minivan. A lot. *Heck Melinda, it's a fricking car!* Yes, I know, but I felt this universal acknowledgment of what it symbolized—lack, pain, hard work, but then abundance and success. Letting that go and starting over was the mountain I had in front of me.

I started seeing more black Tahoes than Toyota Sienna minivans on the road. Was that a sign? Oh, but then Mercedes had to come out with a minivan…that's not cool. That jilted my following the bread crumbs and whole letting it go theory. *You just tossed in a temptation. And a pricey one, too! Not fair. Was this a test?*

I decided for my own mental power that I had to let it go. When it was time to get a new car, it would be time. And that time happened late August 2018, when my gas tank started leaking. I had other issues too, and my mileage was close to 300K miles. Yep, as they say in sales, I was a road warrior. But I needed to solve this issue.

The day I went to the car dealer was a full-on going with my gut day. I didn't think twice, I bought the Tahoe but cried my eyes out saying goodbye out loud to the Toyota. It was grieving at its finest, and who knows who saw me and thought I was daffy. I would have to agree. It was a car. Duct taped gas lid and all. It was time to say goodbye and move on.

On that day, I knew my days as a sales rep would start to be numbered. Energetically, since I was going with the Tahoe, I knew it was a sealed deal. But I made a pact with myself that unless I was ready to quit financially, I would do my best to ride this out and likely get fired when we were meant to break ties.

That day happened on September 11, 2020. A few days over a year from when I purchased my Tahoe.

When Covid-19 started and the world started shutting down March 11, 2020; Key West closed its port for cruise ships, which was the start to further closures. The sales rep game changed. I could feel the tide change. Consumer and boutique owner behaviors, shopping patterns, expectations, started to shift.

For me, it became more and more about awareness. I doubled down on my spiritual studies. Made friends online and became even more interested in spiritual readings and connecting the dots. My ideas started for the *Confidence* books, and I started to get bolder on social media. I started to feel I had nothing to lose. The boutiques I sold to were forced to close during the peak tourist earning season, my husband's business was shut down, and the world had gone in a negative spin between Covid-19 and further political issues, not to mention Black Lives Matter.

The world was in chaos and I felt calm, peaceful, and still. It was an odd unshakeable feeling.

How could that be?

Can YouTube Predict the Future?

The signs started in July. Do you watch any tarot card readers on YouTube? This became my new guilty pleasure. Not soap operas, Netflix, Hulu, or any other TV related time fillers, but tarot card readers; and I listened on my morning walks.

In general, I liked the vibe of the YouTube tarot card readings. And as you have read my previous chapter on tarot readings, you know I was already a tarot card fan and believer. I first found Universal Intuition through Cara Alwill, who I had hired as a coach late 2019 into early 2020. Cara started me down the tarot YouTube path.

I then discovered there were many tarot card readers on YouTube, and switched over to Andrea on Truth Well Told Tarot. I loved her energy, and her readings resonated with what I had going on. They were also resonating for Ryan.

But then it started, "The end was coming!"

This message became consistent and louder by the week. The cards told the same story in different fashions each week. And then when Jaclyn from Universal Intuition started saying the same thing, I knew it was going to happen.

I was about to be fired. And so I was.

The funny thing is, it was such a relief to know it was coming. The card readings prepped me mentally for the day. We had already survived the shutdown and major business loss. We never received government or state aid such as UI, PPP, or SBA Loans.

After what we went through, I had the confidence to know we would be okay.

April, 2021

But there are still some energetic attachment cords. I would love to really understand in the grand scheme of life how important it is to "burn all the boats." I have heard the term many times before. I know Tony Robbins says it. The theory of that expression is that energetically, when you have nothing left to lose, you have everything to gain and all of your focus and attention goes towards your next steps, which then can align with the Universe instead of having mixed messages.

The difficult part is when you hear how other people build successful side hustles and can easily quit their main job. *Why can't that be me? Seriously Universe!*

Breathe.

As I mentioned above, Ryan and I had been down that road before. So I wasn't afraid anymore. It was just a tad bit frustrating, to put it mildly. But was it time to cut the final cords?

The vendor from the initial sales rep days was a main final cord. The owners had been disassociating themselves from the sales reps for many years. We all noticed it. It was a definite lack of leadership and very disappointing to witness. They hired a sales manager to replace one that had been harassing me a few years prior. Her skillset was not of leadership but that of a very good planner. Again, when a company's owners are disconnected, they don't see what's right under their noses. They lost touch with the business and the sales team.

What's the lesson here? It wasn't something I could control. Know what I can control and not control, right? So we all just did the best we could to make some money without alignment with the brand.

In early 2021, the company sent out a contract. We had never had a big contract before, only a sample return agreement. This contract was quite large and obviously written by a lawyer. Most companies of this size do not have a big contract. It's demeaning and doesn't feel good to put demands and restrictions on your sales team when all they are receiving is their commission. It's not even logical, to be honest, and we all knew that.

Every time I went to review the contract, I felt ill. Seriously sick to my stomach. Since I am highly clairsentient, I knew this was a sign. I tried on three occasions to read through the contract, and each time I had the same ill feeling. The contract was wrong and unfair on many levels. I have learned to stand in my power and value myself; this contract was not in alignment and my soul knew it.

So, when two of the three reps (me included) did not sign the contract, without any warning or discussion the vendor held our already earned commission. In case you are wondering, the third rep signed it without reading it because contracts give her anxiety, and now she regrets signing.

Can you say unethical? *Yep.*

Now here's the spiritual part.

Being angry wasn't going to get me anywhere because, as all of us reps had learned, they were leading with ego. They wanted a contract signed that was in their best interest and not their team's best interest.

It was super important to try to protect my energy as much as possible. Not easy, but important.

Lessons Learned

I had a situation happen in the fall with the large rep group I was with. I had learned the hard way, as the large group's contract had a limited time payout agreement which, hence, did not include all my commission earned.

After I was let go, I had someone review the contract I had with them and he said, "Never sign a contract like this. It's purely in favor of the company and not you." I learned my lesson.

It was time again to let go. What was meant to be was meant to be, and if the ride was over, I was okay with that. After not receiving my earned pay and being put on hold without a discussion, who would want to sell this company's product anyways, right?

That realization brought me peace. Balanced my energy and gave me content for this chapter to help others who may be dealing with a situation with a company that is operating in this space.

I ended up using bits of the story for a Facebook Live on making a burn list.

Do Try This at Home: Make a Burn List

It's a nifty and easy thing to do. Take any piece of paper. My piece of paper was from my stationary pad that I mentioned earlier that says, "I want to be like Barbie, that bitch has everything."

Next, write down all of the things that are sucking up your energy. People, situations, companies, even tech issues. *I hate tech issues.* Give it a rest and come back to look at it. I'll bet you may be surprised at how trivial the list is in the grand scheme of things. In my own example, when I reflected back to all that my husband Ryan and I had survived, I knew we would be okay.

Then—BURN IT! I happen to have a gorgeous metal bowl that I use for sage burning. I took it outside, along with some favorite crystals, and set up a little ceremony in my dumpy backyard.

I prayed,

> *Please God, Universe, Spirit Team of the Highest Truth, and Compassion and all the Archangels:*
>
> *Please help rid me of these things I cannot control and have them work out in favor and for the highest good. Thank you! Amen.*

And I burned the piece of Barbie paper and then sent it to Facebook for a post. Done.

I have the chills now, thank you guides!

I went to bed, hoping for the best.

The AP manager emailed me that it was in the hands of the sales manager. Yep, our commissions had intentionally been put on hold. *Stressful!*

And more trust was required from me.

I had gone to the little local beach the day before. I like to go early to meditate, just for an hour. I look at the ocean and clear my head. It is extremely important to have some type of mental clearing practice. Do you have one? Obviously, meditation is great. But also walking or gardening can do the trick, too. Or…just staring at the ocean.

The challenging thing about this beach is that non-locals have found out about it and tend to take over. Somehow (probably via social media) the little spot became public knowledge, and on this day a chatty tourist set up camp right where I was going to relax.

I hate to say it, but it was annoying. Yep, here is my human side. It's a public area so I get it and need to get over myself. But, then it's my choice not to go if I don't want to be bothered. So, during my walk, I debated round and round…

Do I go to the beach to meditate?

Or

Do I stay home to meditate?

You would swear I was trying to create world peace with my internal debate.

I decided to ask. Why the heck not ask? I was torn 50/50 anyway, so I had nothing to lose but maybe a little time with my short drive if I went there, was annoyed, and had to turn around and come home.

Let's see what comes back...

"Yes, go to the beach."

So I went, and was by myself. YAY! *Thank you!!!*

Following the bread crumbs.

Then the day came for the big phone call to discuss the contract and hopefully receive the commission due to me.

I woke up at 4 a.m.; no commission. Standing tall in my power and confidence I emailed, "Unless my commission comes through we are not having a 2 p.m. call."

Miraculously, an email was sent within a half hour stating that the commission had come through. A miracle, divine intervention or someone finally took care of it, who knows. I always give credit to the divine. Why not?

Next up was the call. I have to say, in the past I had a history of getting very heated, and I feel that oftentimes leaders egg people on so that the person can be more on the defensive and then have a bad reaction, which leads to mind loops, etc. I was certain, this time, that I was not going to be that person.

I prayed for extra strength and asked my team for help with these things:

1. Stay Calm.
2. Don't say much.
3. Get off the phone as fast as possible.
4. Hold my ground.

For the most part, I would give myself an A. I held my ground and the call only went over by 10 minutes. The owner and the manager had a habit of talking way too much, which wasted a lot of time and nothing compelling was said. *Truth.* Hence, setting a time boundary is always a good idea when you see a pattern like this. *Tip.*

I only spoke up when necessary or to cut either of them off. I steered clear of anything that could be considered free business advice. I had been down that road before. You need to earn that or pay. Neither was going to be occurring, so I kept it shut and tight.

I asked for help and followed my intuition. Thank you!

Do Try this at Home: Manifesting your Desires

A couple of weeks went by and the situation was still looming. I honestly kept forgetting that I needed to deal with it. Luckily, since I was forgetting, I wasn't having any bad energy or mind loops. I kept busy working on my future intentions. But I still believe there was confusion to the Universe.

One of the top tips of manifesting your dream life, relationship or situation is absolute clarity and energy focus on the direction you desire. Let's face it; this is a tough task when it's wrapped in money needs and desires.

Having an unresolved situation only prolongs the manifestation. This is why things may take longer to manifest. Whether it's a job, relationship, money, etc., when you're all over the board in your thoughts, it is confusing. You are going back and forth in your desires and the energy involved.

It makes sense when you think about it, but we often don't realize this. Another thing to remember is that we as humans are sovereign, meaning we have ultimate control. The Universe needs a clear path to get the job done.

Imagine your intentions as a vacant lot with lots of nasty, dead, thorny weeds in the way. If your guides or the Universe don't have permission to cut them down, they can't help any further because the weeds are in the way.

Hence why clearing triggers, limiting beliefs and any mindset issues are crucial. I won't go into depth about limiting beliefs in this book because I feel so many manifestation and Law of Attraction books cover limiting beliefs. If you need help with limiting beliefs, there are plenty of resources on all platforms.

Once you realize what a limiting belief is, you can catch it when you say it.

Quick examples:

- "I can't afford it."
- "That's only for rich people."
- "That'll never happen."

What are you saying to yourself or to others? Why are you saying it? Nip it in the bud, recognize why you are saying it, change it, rearrange it. The majority of coaches, including myself, cover this when you start working with them or buy their courses. It's an important first step and you may need some help in catching them as they occur. Once you start the process to crush them, it gets easier and more natural.

That being said, I needed to end the situation with that company and move forward. Since I had learned so much and trusted the Universe, I decided to end the relationship when it would inspire me to do so.

What does that mean? I didn't let my human brain tell me when. I let it go until I was naturally inspired by a plan that would come to me at just the right time. And so, it did.

On a Thursday morning walk, out of nowhere, it popped into my brain that that day was the day to end the relationship and to also give an end date of the last day of the month. This was a fair solution I hadn't thought of, so I trusted that since it was coming to me through my intuition, it was a clear path. I sat with it for half of the day and it felt good. I acted on that divine guidance that day with that plan.

And so, it was done.

Gosh, I really love breadcrumbs. So much less pressure to make the "right" decision. I left it up to the Universe to guide me.

The trick is to remember not to be a in rush, and trust.

> "By letting go it all gets done."
> —Lao Tzu

Chapter 7
The Power of "What If"

> "If you assume success and persist in that
> assumption you cannot fail. That is law."
> —Neville Goddard

MANIFESTATION IS ONE OF MY favorite topics. I write about our manifesting story of how we moved to The Florida Keys in *Confidence Mastery for Couples* (CMFC). Some days, I have to pinch myself. Remind myself when things get slow, or I start to doubt my capabilities. I need to remind myself of what I have manifested in the past to remember that it's all possible and keep going.

We all have the power within us. But often, we need reminders. Our human brain clouds those memories, and we have to focus to bring them back. We have to remember to bring them back.

I AM GUILTY OF THIS. I need to remind myself of all the things that we've manifested that have come true. And often, we were doing this before we had even heard the word "manifestation." When I was in college, I said to myself: "I am applying for one college and getting early acceptance. It is done."

That is what happened. I applied to one college, Purdue University, was accepted in the fall of my Senior year and that was it. Again, done.

Companies I desired to work for, Saks Fifth Avenue and Victoria's Secret, hired me Victoria's Secret was part of the Limited Brands, and I didn't care which brand I would get a job with. I had admired the founder, Les Wexner, since I was old enough to understand business and retail. At age 29, I was able to present a product review presentation—an amazing opportunity! I manifested all of that!

Starfish and LLC's

One beautiful Saturday morning, as I was about to plop my butt down in my beach chair for my mediation, I noticed a starfish in the water. So cool! A starfish floating close to shore in The Keys is very rare. It's a gift to see such a magnificent creature. I was happy and awestruck. In all of my beach travels and adventures, I have only ever found a starfish one other time while Ryan and I were on vacation in Roatan, Honduras. I was surprised and delighted!

It led me down memory lane, recalling how I chose our LLC names when we were still living in Minneapolis, MN, and didn't have a clue about where, exactly, we were going or what we were going to do. We had a little plan, but definitely not a HOW. I said to Ryan one day as inspired action hit me over the head, "Let's go to Wells Fargo and set up our future LLCs."

No human told me to do that. I didn't hear it anywhere or read it anywhere. It popped into my brain as an idea for something to do on a cold day. We left the city and drove out to a Wells Fargo Bank branch and walked in, sat down and started the process. I picked the two names. Two Starfish LLC was for Ryan's future business. I loved starfish and was fascinated at how they regenerated. It was the perfect name for his business, as we were starting over.

For my, at the time, future business, I picked the name Two Adirondacks LLC. I was OBSESSED with Adirondack chairs for as long as I could remember.

You know the chairs that have kick-back seating and wide back to them? Often in white or fun colorful colors? I had photographs and greeting cards picturing them on my wall, and one year I had sent Christmas cards with Adirondack chairs. To me, they signified living somewhere warm and being able to sit back and chill. I loved them so much! Again, I was obsessed.

I remember the banker being like, "What is up with these names?" and I had to explain it to him. He probably thought I was a little loo loo. But I didn't care. I was super excited, and it signified a new adventure that would magically unfold. Again, no clue HOW but we took action to set up the two business banking accounts.

We all have manifested many things in our lives. Good and bad. *Yes, you can manifest bad things very easily.* Getting fired, illness, money loss, breakups; you name it, you can create that, too. Many people don't realize what they are creating.

Become aware so you can catch your thoughts and shift them to focus on what you DO want, not what you DON'T want.

Fear and Manifesting

When I officially launched my coaching business in early 2019, I lived in fear of getting found out from the large rep group I represented. When I say I lived in fear, it was severe fear. As 2019 went on, I needed a new car, as mentioned earlier. It had well over 200K miles, and I was proud that my minivan had carried me along. I bought that minivan when I had zero money and was in the process of starting with the large rep group. So, the journey to pay off the minivan was a big one in itself.

But it was time to make a decision. Was I going to get another minivan, which energetically meant that I was committing myself to be a rep even longer, or was I going to buy a Chevy Tahoe—a black, badass Tahoe, to signify my moving on? And then what did that mean? If I bought the Tahoe, energetically was I designing my own demise as a sales rep? And how could I move forward with that knowledge and get out of my head?

Pushing through this limiting mindset was a huge challenge. We all get in our heads, like it or not.

Mind loops can be consuming as we go over the positives and negatives of a situation. We are taught at an early age to review the positives and the negatives, almost in a black and white vacuum. If I were to have done it that way, I would have been focused primarily on the money that being a sales rep provided me. The freedom to not have any emotional pressure on my husband and his business, and the capability to still buy whatever I wanted or go on vacation a couple of times a year.

This is the path many take. Safety. But is it safe in the eyes of the Universe? What does that look like? Because the Universe has us. Our guides are holding us. Looking us in the eye and telling us we will be okay. My vision was bigger than driving around in my car for the rest of my life, peddling someone else's merchandise, receiving a cut, and dealing with a lot of B.S. that sucked my energy and often pissed me off.

With my highest heart and belief in the greatest good, I decided to buy the black Tahoe. I loved the Tahoe. I loved how badass it was. I loved how even when I fell out of it many times, I still felt invincible.

Seriously, I fell out of it on my ass. *Ouch! Did anyone see me? Just a little embarrassing.*

So, what did this mean? It meant I was being guided to start getting ready to leave my sales job. It was the larger company that I had the fear around. The smaller companies were usually pretty good at leaving me alone to manage the energy around that and shift those companies more into side hustle mode, as my time would be greatly freed up.

The larger rep group had been watching my LinkedIn profile, so I knew they were watching me. A bonus of having a premiere account, right? You can see who is watching you. I didn't like repping for the larger group, so that wasn't the issue at all. It was a toxic environment which I picked up on from day one, but I loved the vendors, my fellow reps, and my customers, so I kept my racehorse blinders on and did what I needed to do to service my accounts and make money.

I think it's Tony Robbins that said, "Burn the Boats!" *Yep…*

"If you want to take the island, then burn your boats. With absolute commitment come the insights that create real victory."
—Tony Robbins

This mindset haunts people that have a side hustle. I know it haunted me.

Thank you, Tony, for some help with the confidence!

"What if you are thinking about something you wish to achieve?" I think I first heard that on an Abraham Hicks YouTube video, but I don't recall exactly. You may have likely heard that tip before, too. It's a good one! But are you doing it? If not, let this be your friendly spiritual reminder. I know I need reminders once in a while, so nothing personal. *Sometimes more than once in a while.*

If you don't know that affirmation, here's the scoop! Let's say you desire something, but it may seem like a long shot. And your human mind is stuck on the long shot aspect instead of realizing anything is possible. It happens to the best of us.

So instead of focusing on anything like how, or it's "soooo expensive," or "it'll never happen," Or any of the stuff you say or have heard others say over the years, switch it to "What if?"

What ifs help to shift your thoughts to those that are not loaded with pressure, but instead are fun and happy. You can play with What ifs all day long. I know I have my go-to list that I run through now and again on my morning walk, and even other times if I remember.

Here are a few of mine—feel free to adopt or tweak to get started:

- "What if we had a private chef?"
- "What if we had a beautiful guest house for our friends and family come to stay?"
- "What if we lived part-time in another country?"

Have fun with this! Connect with me on yours and stay tuned for your what ifs to come true. I don't know HOW, but they will.

Putting It Out There

Another part of manifesting that I strongly believe in is speaking it into existence.

Have you ever done that? It's fun, and as long as you don't negate the energy by thinking that you are lying, it actually works. These stories will also merge with being or embodying vs. just doing. Something I have to remind myself of from time to time.

Here are some examples regarding our small business Good Karma Sportfishing.

Baggies! Yep, gallon-sized zip lock baggies. I purchase baggies often. Yes, we need them for the business. But not all the time. I made it a practice years ago always to buy the large gallon zip lock baggies whenever I am at Walmart because in my mind I tell myself, "Ryan gets booked all the time and always catches large fish, so he needs larger size baggies."

Did we have a lot of boxes of baggies when we first started our business? "Yes!" However, it worked out and now he is booked every day and always catches large fish.

For many years, I had a sales customer who was very kind, and always asked me how our business was. It was a very good store in Fort Myers, and I really liked the two owners.

They asked out of kindness vs. many other people who asked out of thinking, or even dare I say hoping, we would fail. I could always feel the energy difference when he inquired, "How's your husband's business doing?"

From the early stages I would always say, "Great! Thank you for asking! He has fishing charters booked every day!"

I had a twinge of guilt for not necessarily telling the whole truth. However, I shifted my mindset and pushed through those thoughts. After a few short years, he did end up getting booked every day. We have raised our rates so many times I have lost track. We recently eliminated the shortest charter and cheapest charter option to be able to adjust to supply and demand.

Try it!

My Sales Business—Embody It!

Another thing I used to do when I started as a sales rep was to fully embody the sales rep title. We still did not have a pot to piss in, but in my mind, I was a successful sales rep.

I used to attend the local women's business group for their monthly luncheons. Ryan and I had just moved to The Florida Keys and I was struggling with figuring out how to make any money in sales. I was repping the so-called company based overseas, and it was a nightmare. At the monthly luncheons, with about 50 in attendance on average, we had to go around the room and stand up to introduce ourselves.

Oh geez, the skin-tingling anxiety that I had to overcome and push through was incredible. However, I had faith and each month proudly stood up, held my head high, choked back any negative limiting beliefs and said, "My name is Melinda Van Fleet, and I am an independent sales rep."

I would promptly sit back down, breathe, and pray no one asked too many questions or questions I couldn't answer. Now I understand that working through that energy sooner would have likely brought The Law of Attraction into effect sooner, but at least I was on the right path.

It took a solid three years for my business to take off and bring home over six figures, but I kept going and saying out loud, "I am a successful independent sales rep."

During my travels in South Florida, which tends to be quite hot in the summer months, I never focused on the heat or all of the challenges like many of the other reps did.

In my mind, I was a very successful sales rep, and even if someone didn't buy from me that time on that visit, they would buy another time. I mentally put myself in a position of achieving high sales and shut out all the other noise. I envisioned and embodied it every day.

Of course it was going to happen!

I kept my eye on the prize, my head down and kept building my confidence that I would achieve success.

You can do this, too!

> "Diamonds are nothing more than chunks of coal that stuck to their jobs."
> —Malcom Forbes

Chapter 8

Your Soul's Journeys

"The only impossible journey is the one you never begin."
—Tony Robbins

How awakened are you to your soul's journey?

I ask you this because I think about it often. Whenever I have a trigger or something happens in general, I have trained my mind to think of the person or situation from their perspective. It takes work and remembering to do it in the moment. I first heard the phrase "see yourself as others" from Gabby Bernstein, and have mentioned it before on podcasts. It's a good reminder to take a moment and try to put yourself in another's shoes and consider what they may have occurring in their life.

Some of you may already understand that and think this way. But, I would bet that most people do not think about their souls' journey or other people's soul journey. As humans, we judge ourselves and others, get angry, sad, frustrated, etc. But what if you took the pressure off and changed your mindset to think about it as their journey?

And I am still learning…

I had something happen to me yesterday that I am still reeling from. Today is March 11, 2021. I like to note the date because establishing a point in time as a reference is essential to the growth journey. I would recommend this if you journal. It's amazing to go back in a few years and be like, "Wow, I cannot believe I am still doing this." OR hopefully, "Wow, I have grown so much!"

My first book, *Confidence Mastery for Couples (CMFC)*, launched March 9th. I consider myself a fairly balanced person. It's one of my superpowers. I am well aware that not everyone will like or resonate with what I write. It's what makes the world go round—different opinions, values, etc.

Also, I am aware that someday I may have a hater or someone who wants to take their own issues out on me. What is it they say, "You know you made it when you have a hater." But what happened was from a context of ego. Someone I love and who should support me without even another thought did something from their ego, not from a place of pure intentional love. And not only did it cause me to go through the full range of emotions—laughter, then pissed, then sadness. It fucked with my marketing and also my energy. Not cool and yes, I used the f-word.

The laughter in my first reaction was because I knew the why behind what happened. "Oh, that's so them." My generous nature was to be accepting of that person's behavior. This, however, is what happens when you are a people pleaser and not good with setting boundaries or standing up for yourself. Which, as we all know, is not right. In the end, that doesn't feel good, and you are still dealing with a situation, likely having mind loops and continuing the story.

Then I started to get pissed because of the marketing and how it messed up my plan, which was not only for my purposes but was also to help support others. I would have tagged other people in the marketing post in question. Being pissed doesn't help either, as you are not releasing the emotions. Anger continues to be stored until, like some people, you blow up at someone else who is undeserving or punch a hole in the wall. I am sure we all have stories which come to mind.

The more I started to think about the situation and the layers, the more I realized how unfortunate it was that this person operated this way. Sad for me and the reflection, and sorry for them. I needed to stop burying my sadness. As a strong Aries with an old male soul, I am good with burying the shit and moving on. One may think this is admirable, but if it festers at the subconscious level as sadness, creating a blue ring around me. That is not good.

Keeping all that sadness buried doesn't help. Long-term it can also cause health issues such as back pain, neck pain, headaches, heart pain, etc., and many people do not realize that. In addition, people can feel sadness as energy.

Let's be real; who wants to be around sad people? When you read someone's sad post on Facebook, does it feel good to you? You may politely comment because you have compassion, but you don't want that same energy. Hence why it's critical to move through sadness and pain to try to get to the other side.

As the day went on, my head started swirling with all of the layers of this situation. I lost the rest of my productive day. My day went down the tubes. Then that pisses me off, as I thrive on being productive and have a lot to do. So, I decided to call this person. When I did, I was spot on with my reckoning, which I knew I was. The conversation went as I expected. I was prepared for an excuse and a half apology.

Okay, so this is life. Sorry to break it to you, but it is. How many of you can think of something that has happened where you went through an emotional cycle and landed in a place where you knew you were right, but there was nothing you could do about it? You cannot change another person. I hear stories about this all day long from coaching clients. The hard part is that if you turn a blind eye and become someone who coasts along and doesn't address your issue externally (with the other person) or internally, it rears its ugly head again. It's crucial to make a change one way or another.

What to do? I will break down my thought process, and you can pull out what resonates with you.

1. I chose to be at peace with their soul's path being ego focused. Again, I cannot change them. Their patterns in life repeat.
2. I chose to realize that I did not want to be like that, and to be even more conscious than I already am about the choices I make going forward. I approached them with full positivity.
3. I chose to keep focused on the good that was happening around me; celebrating all of the wins along the way.
4. I reminded myself of the urgency of staying on the positive path from an energic standpoint. Getting sucked down into the muck of feeling bad could hurt my book and my business, which in turn hurts my intention to help others with my stories, teachings, and message.
5. I had a breakdown moment while walking my youngest shih tzu, Miracle (yep, a dog walking moment again as in CMFC), and got the sadness out of me. I had to push through my shell and allow myself to cry for an hour to get rid of the sadness in my energy field.

Combining these tools—energy, understanding we are souls in this lifetime, emotional reckoning, knowing how you wish to be, all together take your journey to the next level so you can be your best person for yourself and others.

I would also recommend a Soul Plan Reading with Bella Luna. I had my reading with Bella right before I was finished writing this book. I share the details in The Good Karma Success Coach Podcast Episode 132. It's the most mind freeing experience to know you are living your soul plan. Bella walks you through the dynamics of how your challenges, talents, and goals all work together towards your destiny.

The morning I am writing this, I woke up feeling kind of "meh." After my morning meditation and energy clearing, I pulled an oracle card from Colette Baron-Reid's *Oracle of the 7 Energies* deck (published by Hay House). I love this oracle deck! The cards are gorgeous, and the messages are on point.

Wouldn't you know the card I pulled was card #28-Broken Open, which says:

"There are situations in life where you see the value of loss, grief, and a broken heart…No, not even the story of what happened, the details surrounding what has brought you to your knees, is as important as what *results* from the experience."

I think the oracle card paints a picture, no?

Chapter 9
Why Can't They?

> "In the end, only three things matter: how much
> you loved, how gently you lived and how gracefully
> you let go of things not meant for you."
> —Buddha

AS I MENTIONED IN CHAPTER 8, the concept of "see yourself as others" was life changing for me. However, since not everyone reads every word or hears every piece of content, nor do they remember or practice #truth, it bears repeating. I believe there is also always a lesson in repeating. Tony Robbins is a master at repeating. When you repeat a message, the message sinks in.

In addition, it's interesting how often a coach may talk about something, but until you are ready to hear it, it's as if your brain tunes it out. Maybe it's from our childhoods when our parents wanted us to do something we didn't want to do. I would guess that we all have a few of those stories, right? Stories where if you lived somewhere where it snowed, like me, and your mom was always nagging you to "bundle up" when it snowed, and you didn't want to bundle up. But, then you move out of the house, go away to college in Indiana, and upon the first snowstorm where you have to walk 30 minutes to class, you realize, G*eez, mom was right, it would be nice to have some long underwear and a hat.* I think you get my point.

So often, we get frustrated and in a mind loop of why can't they? "Why can't they just do it?" You may even add the "f word" in there sometimes. *I do.*

It's pretty amazing how you can get yourself all in a tizzy (channeling my grandma here) about what someone else is or isn't doing. You cannot control them. You may try to control them, but you can't. You can politely suggest. I would hope that you would do so "politely." However, I fall victim to being demanding on occasion. Truth—work in progress!

Gosh, why do we hindsight ourselves with all the things we could have done better?

Why? Because we are not perfect. *Gasp!!!*

When I had my soul reading with Debbra Lupien, it opened my eyes to understanding that we are all at different levels. This thought process and learning also ties in with the previous chapter. Our souls have lived thousands of lives before. And some souls are older than others. The reading clicked in my brain the dynamics of what this means. Not from an arrogant place, but from a place of understanding and awareness that some folks may just not be there yet. Maybe they will learn in this lifetime, or perhaps they won't.

And again, I cannot control what they learn in this lifetime.

See how that works? For the majority of people, we only know what we know in this lifetime. But your soul advances, as well. Depending on what you do with your time, and the work you do on yourself (mindset), you will be advancing in this lifetime.

You can also bundle in your experiences, behaviors, and relationships. I even take this to the level of being competitive. If someone is "ahead of you," once you come to a place of understanding someone else's journey vs. yours, and it's something you can't control, there is no reason to be envious. The other person is ahead of you, for whatever reason; maybe their soul started on becoming before yours did. If we all looked at our competitive or envious behaviors that way, it would take so much pressure off, and we could enjoy our life's journey.

Freedom from triggers, envy, and competition. Nice, huh? Try that mindset shift on for size.

It's Okay—Friends Come and Go

I will share a tremendous real-life example regarding letting go of control. Someone I know (let's call her Sue) was married to a guy who was controlling, narcissistic, judgmental, etc. They were married for over 20 years. For 20 years she painfully dealt with his behavior, was miserable and stressed out at times, and finally dared to leave. Sue became a whole new person! She laughed, had fun, relaxed, and did the things she wanted to do. Unfortunately, Sue was also lonely and missed being married. She missed committing to another person. Sue dated various men. She was in love for a time with someone who couldn't commit, which was painful and she had to walk away. Sue dated some more and finally met someone she felt she could settle down with. The challenge that showed up for everyone knowing the situation was that the new husband, except for a few aspects, was extremely similar to the previous husband. It was as if the clock had been set back. It was as if she was in a time warp. She was repeating the same behavior by marrying the same type of controlling, negative energy, judgmental person.

In all honesty, as an outsider, it sucks. It sucks to see someone go backward. Plus, it's no fun for me or the other people involved to spend that much time with Sue anymore, because she is always with her new husband. Yes, that is selfish, but true. Here's the thing, I need to be happy, too. My energy is affected by people that are not aligned with how I like to see and behave in the world. So, if it's yucky to be around Sue and her new husband, I have to move on as best as I can.

This is not the first time someone I am friends with married someone I didn't like.

Years ago, I was good friends with someone when I moved to Minneapolis, MN. I considered her a best friend. But then she married her husband, who was not as pleasant. They came to visit us in The Keys on two occasions.

After the second visit, Ryan said, "No more. He is nasty, demanding, controlling, and not even kind or friendly to our dogs." Ryan was correct. He was a nasty person, and if you are not nice to our three-little shih tzus, we have to move on.

It was sad to let her friendship go, but since we lived so far from each other, I considered her friendship a point in time. She had also had a hard time finding a husband, so I doubt she was going to leave him to start over. I understand the behavior. As I wrote about in CMFC, I didn't get married to Ryan until I was almost 35 years old, and we definitely had our share of growing pains.

We all have similar situations. Some of us have more confidence to spend less time with that person or even walk away. In the case of Sue, it's spending less time. I can't fully walk away. Why? Because I can see why Sue did what she did, and I am at a different stage in my life. However, I spend less time with her in order to manage my energy and stay in alignment.

I understand that it will be Sue's pattern to repeat in this lifetime or the next lifetime until she has the courage to not attach to someone who has bad energy. Again, I cannot control who someone chooses to marry. I can only "see myself as the other person" and be at peace with her choice. Trying to control someone or a situation doesn't feel good. It goes against our nature, and frankly, rarely works. You will spend more time trying to control, then letting go, walking away, or giving space. Sometimes people come to the realization on their own that they should have done or said something else. But sometimes they don't. Ryan and I have several standing "jokes."

One is, "A jerk doesn't wake in the morning thinking they are a jerk." Think about it. Who do you know that wakes up and says, "What a great day! I am going to be my jerky self today!"

We deal with "the jerk mentality" all the time. *Yep, I am calling it out and giving it a name.* How did we come up with this? Because once in a while, luckily not often, Ryan will have a bad client on a fishing charter. Some have been bad. I like to go to the marina to help after a charter, because I can witness some of the behavior firsthand to help Ryan move through it because the behavior can be so triggering.

I will never forget this one couple from Miami. They were extremely demanding on catching fish vs. relaxing and having fun. They left the boat a mess with their trash; not putting it in the garbage can like most clients do. She was dictating to Ryan how to clean the fish, they didn't tip, and they were overall unappreciative. The trip itself was an outstanding success with a large catch of high-quality good sized fish. My husband takes extra care in cleaning the fish, removing all of the small bones and bloodlines. Most captains don't do this extra step, as it takes more time. I was at the marina and met them; I couldn't believe how they were behaving. My mama bear wanted to push the wife in the water. *Yep, not a good idea, right?*

Anyhow, the crazy thing is, you would think they were saying to themselves they had a terrible time and would never fish with Ryan again. But nope, they called the next week to book another charter.

Seriously.

Blocked.

See, jerks don't often think they are jerks.

Bless them and let them go.

We stopped ourselves from going down an energy path of, "Why can't they?" "Why didn't they?" and moved on. They were not going to change, and we could not make them change. When you see yourself as others and realize their soul's journey is at that level, it takes off the pressure and you can allow yourself to move forward in the way that makes you happy. *I like to be happy; you?*

Arrogance vs. Knowledge

I also had to let go of thinking I was arrogant or that the knowledge I was gathering was from a place of ego. Over the years, I have noticed that many people are quick to say, "you are full of yourself" or "what you say is ego-based."

I have let that soak in too much, as I am very critical of myself. Self-judgment. I would dare to lay bets it's a pattern from childhood that's held over into adulthood, as most things are.

Do you have that, too? Self-judgment?

It's been a challenge for me to move past that; as it has been to reverse patterns. In other words, maybe there was something I didn't think I was doing at all, then someone's content made me think I was doing it and I would start to doubt myself. All mind loops that go on that no one talks about. This pattern came up in one of my readings with Margo Parks, and she helped me to break it. It's nice to have someone to safely share your inner thoughts with. I intend to always do the same.

> "Sometimes letting go is an act of far greater
> power than defending or hanging on."
> —Eckart Tolle

Chapter 10

Obsessed with Human Design

> "Human Design is a mental system, so we can finish
> our mental business and get to the spirit. We can't
> get to the spirit until we finish this mind trip."
> —Ra Uru Hu

OVER THE YEARS, PRIMARILY WHEN I worked in the corporate world, I have taken many personal development exams. Companies have an HR department, a budget, and then they often hire a trainer from the company to come in, have employees take an exam, give a lecture and leave. I wrote about HBDI in CMFC, as that was one personal development exam that stuck with me, and I applied the learnings.

Would you agree on the fact that if you find at least one good nugget in a book or personal development test, it's a win? The same goes for a recipe book. I think I first heard the theory with recipes. It seemed odd to me at the time, but now after reading so many books over the years, I would tend to agree.

With Human Design, it's been a different ball game. If you don't know what Human Design is, I will share some topside information so that you understand when I dive in with the stories.

Human Design is a system that combines metaphysical methodologies (such as Chakras, Kabbalah, Astrology, and Quantum Physics) to help people make shifts in their consciousness so they can evolve. The system was downloaded from The Divine to Robert Alan Krakower in 1987. Robert later changed his name to Ra Uru Hu.

I would highly recommend the following books and websites if you wish to learn more.

- *Understanding Human Design* by Karen Curry
- *Understanding Your Clients Through Human Design* by Robin Winn, MFT
- www.humandesignamerica.com
- www.freehumandesignchart.com

There is a lot more depth in those resources than anything I will be covering here. So, I recommend the above books and websites to learn more. The two books have been the basis of my learning, and the information has pulled out to draw conclusions in relation to my experiences.

When I received a reading by Margo Parks in the Fall of 2020, I had never heard of Human Design. Now, I feel it's like the car manifesting theory I am sure you have heard. "If you desire a Black Range Rover, all of the sudden, they are everywhere you look." *Exaggerating a little bit, but not about the Range Rovers; they are everywhere in South Florida.*

What drew me in immediately was how relatable and accurate this concept is. I could take the test for free and receive results which I could directly apply. All I needed to do was enter my birth information.

A busy person like me loves that! No complicated thinking questions that spin you around. *Thank you Ra Uru Hu and The Divine!*

I am a 3/5 Pure Generator. Learning about my Human Design Type helped shed a lot of light on who I am and how I behave. I have always been an action taker and thrive on being busy. The busier I am, the more productive I become. When I am not busy, I tend to fall into what I refer to as a "slack pit." I never feel good in the slack pit, which means I am unaligned with my true self. *Mystery solved!*

I have always been amazed and even judged (unfairly, to be honest) people that sit around and watch TV all day because I have never been "that person." I would make fun of people that hang in the slack pit. Certainly not a kind way to be, and when I reflect upon my judgment, I feel ashamed and embarrassed. There are other types such as Projectors and even Reflectors who require more self-care-related rest and a break from other types, such as a Generator like myself. *Now that I understand, I can't say I blame them. I would want a break from me, too.*

Having even a basic understanding using the Human Design system freed up so much mind space and created awareness to let not only judgment of others but also self-judgment go.

Alignment feels amazing!

Busy Bee

It's amazing how some memories can stick with you and others you forget. One such memory is when I lived in Downtown Chicago. I had a good number of friends and was in the Chicago Social Club, a large organized quarterly sporting (and we did our fair share of drinking) organization, and worked two jobs. I was very busy and extremely happy.

Except for the lack of a boyfriend, and living beyond my means, I would say I was pretty darn lucky with my lifestyle. However, my mother judged my busy schedule. She would often say, "There are no awards at the end of the day for being the busiest person." I thrived on being busy, so her judgment was an annoying trigger.

Even when I was in my corporate job as a buyer, slow times would drive me crazy. I would end up wasting the day away talking to co-workers and taking a long lunch. I would feel worse on those days vs. days I was crazy busy and some people would assume it was stressful. To me, it wasn't stressful at all; I loved it!

When I was a full-time sales rep, my happiest days were when I had all the lines available with a large multi-vendor rep group I represented at the time and six other side-lines. But, as luck would have it, the rep group cut my package in half for their own benefit, leading me down a path of finding more purpose and fulfillment and asking the Universe, "What's next?" I have a note on my bulletin board dated 3/17/17 asking, "What is Next?"

And here we are. Ask and you shall receive.

When you have even the simplest clarity that results from knowing your type, the pressure you put on yourself, as well as statements others make, fall to the wayside. *Ahhh…what a great relief.*

Yes, I'll Take Another

Another self-discovery busted a nasty trigger which would rear its head every once in a while. I tended to get annoyed when someone else shared an idea with me. Their idea would work well, and then I would be annoyed that it wasn't my idea. This thought process and trigger may sound odd to you, but people don't normally share the ugly thoughts they have because of fear of judgment. When I learned that a characteristic of being a Generator to is take action on other people's ideas and suggestions, or that waiting to have something all come together before acting were the best forms of successful action for my type, I felt like throwing a massive party with a lot of cake! *I love cake with extra icing. I am making myself hungry.*

And then guess what? Who is one of the most famous people in the world? Most likely in the Top 10 of when asked the question, "Who would you like to have dinner with?"

Can you guess? I will give you a moment...

Yes, it's Oprah. Oprah is a Generator. *How cool is that? Oprah and I are in the same club! Do you want my autograph now?*

It makes sense. If you think about the fact that she built an incredible life (and dare I also mention fortune) on building relationships, interviewing other people, and sharing their success, which then helps millions of people. *Well, that pretty much took away any triggers related to being upset about other folks' ideas. I am good now, rolling on!*

Understanding Others

My husband, Ryan, is a Manifesting Generator. Since it is easy to find out other peoples' types, I recommend running the chart for anyone else in your life with whom you desire to have a better relationship or even if you are just curious about them.

For years, I have told my husband he is a Jedi. Ryan is likely Yoda in human form. I am not kidding. For years, I have intuitively known this to be true. In my synopsis, Manifesting Generators are like Jedis. They have the power to manifest along with the energy a Generator has, so magical shit can happen. On the flip side, I have learned that Ryan can also be his own worst enemy. If he lets self-doubt, triggers, or sadness get a hold of him, his powers do not actualize. As his wife, it is a frustrating experience that often leads to a big discussion and me playing a lot of Abraham Hicks for him on YouTube. Truth!

I find it fascinating to learn some of the challenges that Manifesting Generators have and then correlate them to my own triggers or areas where I have seen a deficit. For example, one of the challenges is skipping steps. Ryan used to be a quality control supervisor for production plants. He was responsible for QA and cleaning. However, at home, he is the one who leaves the dirty rag on the floor. *Cleaning and dirty rag on the floor?* I would laugh, as I was always curious if he did that at work, hence why he had various work challenges.

He also gets burned out after a stretch of charters and needs to recharge. Naps are also something Ryan needs after he "go go goes" hard at getting things done; often various tasks at the same time. Hence, another trait which makes sense knowing how he operates.

Since my initial dive into the Human Design concept, I continue to pick up tidbits here and there and apply them to my life. The learnings help settle my mind and provide such amazing clarity. I have found that understanding Human Design, in conjunction with my Soul Introduction Reading with Debbra Lupien, brings peace to my busy brain and takes my self-judgment down a major notch. It also helps when you know something about yourself, and you may be frustrated if another person does not behave in the same way. They likely are not wired as you are.

I recorded a podcast episode on The Good Karma Success Coach Podcast Episode 122 in which I shared my experience manifesting using Human Design. I put out into the Universe at the end of the podcast to be connected with a Human Design Advisor. As great fortune would have it, it occurred. Yay! You guessed it! Through a fellow writer, Danielle, I was introduced to Human Design Advisor and fellow Life Coach Ann Smyth. Ann shared further incredible insight on my design chart and was a guest on podcast Episodes 130 and 134. All three podcasts are enlightening episodes to listen to, but pull your chart first!

So much of this understanding is simple, but we don't practice it. The judgment rolls around first and then you have to remind yourself, "Hey, they may not be a communicator and have a defined head center;" an example I find when working with someone who isn't naturally inclined to create content.

I love relating Human Design Types to others. It's fascinating how you can assimilate writing styles, topics, and even how another author may handle their book writing and social media based on what type they are. As humans, we judge each other, but when you know it's their type and how they are wired, the acceptance becomes inevitable.

Life & Love Lessons

You can see how having an understanding of Human Design can open your eyes to learning and understanding more about yourself and others, as well.

"Human Design opens the door to the potential of self-love, a love of life, and the love of others through understanding."
—Ra Uru Hu

Chapter 11

I Give Myself Permission

> "To be a great champion you must believe you are
> the best. If you're not, pretend you are."
> —Muhammad Ali

I LIKE TO REFER TO affiliate links as being invited to the party. In the Fall of 2020, one of my fellow author friends, Nicole, posted an affiliate link for *My Million Dollar Experiment*. Who doesn't stop at a post like that? Well, maybe some people, but I surely did. I clicked on the link, saw it was $25 for a year, read about a minute's worth of what it was about, and signed up. Call me crazy, but I take action. *Especially regarding manifesting millions! How fun!*

That click and $25 spend put me into the world of Joanna Hunter, a spiritual business coach based in Scotland. I asked her to be a guest on The Good Karma Success Coach Podcast, Episode 100, in November, and she accepted. If you listen to the episode, know that we easily talked for double the amount of time that was aired. I learned that we had a lot in common; from our joint passion for tarot and oracle cards to family struggles.

I found that I appreciated Joanna's teaching style and it was helping me validate a lot of inner thoughts and feelings I was working through. Some good thoughts and some challenging thoughts.

Sometimes an affirmation, word of validation, relatable story, or tool is all you need to make a significant shift in your mindset and life. I always remember when the shift happens, and I am grateful.

One of those shifts happened in early 2019 when I enrolled in Amanda Frances's Money Mentality Makeover. Amanda Frances is a money manifesting coach who has a variety of online courses.

I have always had good thoughts about money, have been a good manifestor, and at that time I didn't feel limiting beliefs, such as "that's only for rich people," or "keep dreaming" were an issue as much as they been had in the past. Sure, limiting belief creepers happen now and again, but for the most part since we had already been through an extreme job change and moving to The Florida Keys, I had worked on understanding limiting beliefs and shifted my mindset. Since we accomplished what we had so far with Good Karma Sportfishing, I knew that big dreams were possible.

However, I struggled with feeling safe earning money in my sales business while I worked on my coaching business. Shifting that feeling was a huge struggle for me. I had this constant paranoia and was always looking over my shoulder. I was afraid I was going to be fired. In sales, often companies are very strict about focus. They want to make sure their sales reps are 100% focused on their business. And if they find out they are not 100% focused on their business, "Adios amigo!" In English, "Goodbye friend!" Some days it would consume me, and this fear would keep me small and full of anxiety.

One day, while I was intently watching Amanda's videos on my treadmill, one of the other clients on the FB Live had posted a question regarding the same challenge I was having. The woman was also struggling with fear and anxiety about losing her job while building another business as a side hustle.

Amanda gave advice in terms of an affirmation. I perked up, hopped off the treadmill as fast as I could, grabbed my journal, and quickly wrote in my journal my form of the affirmation "I am safe making money in my sales business while I work on my coaching, speaking and writing business," which allowed me something to grab onto when I felt that fear creeping up. That was more than likely what kept money coming in until The Universe and I had more time to get things lined up.

Hearing this affirmation and committing it to memory relieved the pressure and anxiety. It was also comforting that I wasn't alone in this mental business challenge. A huge weight was lifted off my shoulders and I could easily move forward.

Circling back to Joanna Hunter, I had a similar awakening which caused an entire mindset shift. Joanna often says in her videos, and we say it along with her with our hand over hearts, "I give myself permission."

Think about that affirmation. Really do a deep dive. What are you energetically holding yourself back from because you haven't fully given yourself permission to accept, love, move forward on, appreciate, etc.? When I started to embrace this affirmation, more and more thoughts began to appear for which I wasn't giving myself permission. There was a gap in my energy, where I wasn't giving myself permission. And even if it was something I had come to terms with and accept, taking it one step further along the path helped seal the gap even more.

I mentioned in *Confidence Mastery for Couples (CMFC)* that I wasn't owning the success of Good Karma Sportfishing. I always thought of the business as Ryan's, even though he always shared the success with me and I worked with him. This was an important gap to recognize because it's connected to energetics and manifesting. Having this affirmation to hang onto helped me to shift the way I saw the business.

I give myself permission to be a successful piece of Good Karma Sportfishing.

Another example is that I was always judging my Good Karma Success Coach podcast after I recorded and listened to it. I was judging myself and how often I said, "Super excited."

I thought I sounded like an idiot, and I would get upset and therefore be sending bad energy towards my podcast.

In the fall of 2020, I listened to a few other podcasts and realized that these very successful podcasters and coaches said the same thing. And also, so did Joanna!

I give myself permission to be super excited and not care that I happen to say it a lot.

My podcast listens started to grow.

Same with my brand overall—Good Karma Success Coach. I picked that name back in 2018 when I was in coaching class. Obviously, it's an offshoot of our Good Karma Sportfishing Business. Good Karma Success Coach made sense to me, and I was excited about the brand. I didn't think anything more of the name until I took a very high-ticket speaking program in the spring of 2019 that was more B-to-B (Business to Business) than B-to-C (Business to Consumer).

The coaching instructor made me feel small and foolish; like I should hide the brand Good Karma Success Coach and pick another name to better market myself and my services. I also doubted my choice of branding colors, which are my favorite colors, orange and raspberry, my photos, and the layout.

His comments and lack of positive feedback weren't meant to intentionally mess with my head. He certainly had no idea the damage he was doing to my internal energy. However, the thought of not being a very marketable brand, especially since I was so new and didn't know any better, took a nice comfy seat in my subconscious and kicked off its shoes to stay a while. It stayed with me throughout 2019 and into 2020. I had a painful mind loop on replay that also lead me down a path of hiring other coaches to get feedback. None of which worked and caused more stress and anxiety. I wasted so much time, money, and energy. Talk about utter frustration!

Finally, through doing the inner work and using the tools and teachers I had discovered, I found the confidence to break free of this painful story and love my brand. I learned that comparison is not a bad thing. Comparing yourself with someone who is ahead of you can help build confidence.

"If they can do it, you can do it too!" Right?

Often, we think of comparison as only being envy or competition based, but that is not always accurate. It can be used for good! Now, the thought is kicked out and homeless. *See ya!*

It's been a painful journey thinking through all of the energetic missteps. I know the Universe doesn't look at anything as a mistake, only learnings for yourself and to help others. Coaching other women on this mindset is important to me. Once you see direct results from a new mindset, you'll be eager to create a new, empowered pattern. Then you'll be grateful for the learning opportunity created through your mistake. Shifting your mindset that there are no mistakes only lessons to help you grow is a huge win.

> "Your great power lies not on the surface,
> but deep within your being."
> —Roger McDonald

Chapter 12

The Vision Board Quest

> "Create the highest, grandest vision possible for your life because you become what you believe."
> —Oprah Winfrey

I don't recall when I first began loving hearing about other people's purchases. I call it "purchase viewing."

Some people think I am nuts when I ask them, "What did you get for Christmas?"

They respond, "Oh, stuff."

"No, really, I want to know."

I love to hear about gifts. I love giving gifts, receiving gifts, and hearing about the gifts other people have received.

And that's how I feel about Vision Boards. A Vision Board is one big Christmas list (Please note, I am using Christmas as an example, but I realize not everyone celebrates Christmas so please substitute the celebration of your choice). It's fun to pick out what you want from the guy in the big red suit and imagine him delivering it to you on Christmas morning. And that's exactly what it is: fun!

If you are someone who has a Vision Board, you likely understand this feeling. Cutting or tearing out the pretty pictures of your desires is fun, and you should get a great feeling as you do it. If you are not feeling good in the process, and your feeling goes more towards anxiety about not having the money to purchase such an item, hold off on this activity for the moment. Mindset work is what's needed instead, and only you can own up to how you are feeling.

Growing up without spirituality, the internet, books, etc. I had never heard of a Vision Board until I was in my late twenties. One of my favorite things as a child was to go to Downtown Chicago with my family. We were lucky, and to my child self's timeline, we went often. My parents were from the South Side of Chicago, and my mom and dad loved taking drives and going to everything from museums to Marshal Fields every Christmas to see the windows and sit under the big tree. We also attended larger events at the convention center, The Taste of Chicago, Navy Pier, the North Avenue Beach or Lincoln Park Zoo.

To this day, driving along Lake Shore Drive gives me positive chills. The beautiful lake, the buzz of the people outside and how happy they look biking, rollerblading, or walking, Buckingham Fountain, and the tall, pretty buildings. I always had an amazing feeling going downtown. I am feeling high vibes typing this now. Pretty amazing. I wish that as a kid I had known the impact of positive chills and what that really meant for manifesting.

I was fascinated by the boats. I wanted a boat. The funny thing is that as long as I can remember, I have gotten car sick. I had many occasions of puking my guts out or being car sick when the weather conditions were a bit off, so of course I also get boat sick. Nonetheless, I wanted a boat. My parents, especially my mom, would say, "Keep dreaming kid, boats are expensive and no one really uses their boats anyways." Even at a young age, it amazed me that she would try to talk me out of something that someday, when I had my own money, would be none of her business. This went on every time I would say something about boats.

Fast forward to my twenties. I am going through folders and finding magazine pages that I had torn out over the years as a child. I always loved magazines! Being able to get a subscription to a magazine when I was in my early teens was a coming of age moment. The fun happy pictures, tips, pretty models, trendy clothes; all things I aspired to and made me happy. Somewhere in my magazine journey, I had ripped out a picture of a boat and stuck it in the folder. I still have it in my file cabinet. So now, let's see, how many years later did I finally have a boat? Seems crazy, but at the age of when I tore that photo out of the magazine until now, who would have thought? And if I would have paid attention to my parents' mindset, I would have never kept on my true path.

Dreaming as a kid is so important. Why do parents shut down their kids' dreams? I see, hear and read about it all the time. I am also finding more generational gaps in this. As a Gen X-er, I think we had a lot of it. Were our Baby Boomer parents wired to shut things down? Did that come from their parents? Now, we are awakening more to the fact we don't have to follow those generational patterns. We can break them, set boundaries, and lovingly say, "No thanks."

There is a lot of wisdom in understanding that kids dream; and often, kids have an invisible playmate. Scientifically, what if there is any way to prove the invisible playmate is a spirit or a spirit guide? But, I am assuming so. Call me crazy, that's okay, but to me it makes sense. Kids can see things adults can't because their minds are not yet crowded with all the bullshit and noise of the world. The news media, money challenges, fear, judgment, work or business strains, and people triggers have not come into their little worlds yet, so they have an openness to dreaming and possibly; even a spiritual being showing a presence only they can see. *Wow, I wish I knew then that I know now, right?*

I started to think about this in relation to my two nieces; Sienna who is 15 and Sydney Bryn who is 12 years old.

In December of 2020, my intuition guided me to update my Vision Board. I tried to remember when I had last updated it and believe the date to be July 2019. The board followed me around the house, but I never paid much attention to it. It wasn't like I was sitting staring at it, or meditating with it. *Now that I think about it, it may be fun to dance around it and chant.*

It followed me around because I just felt like it was in the way no matter where it was, and so I needed to move it. Since, in my opinion, nothing had changed, I didn't pay it much mind. The main things on my board had to do with our dream house along with all the fixings, and success-related handwritten note cards. None of which had actualized yet, so again I felt like I knew what was on it and kept walking by without really focusing on it.

However, when I finally took the time to look at it, I realized something was on it that had come to fruition. Something I had completely forgotten that I had put on the board. Weight loss. I had written on a notecard, "Nothing tastes as great as skinny feels." I had received that idea from Terry Savelle Foy and her book *Dream It, Pin It, Live It*, which is a fun book to read. The skinny quote was polarizing, it stopped me in my tracks when I read it, so I thought what the heck, lets write it on a notecard and put it on the board. I had no idea what skinny would feel like, but I knew what a bag of Oreos and Cadbury Carmello Candy Bars tasted like, so what the heck, why not? I had a calm, carefree attitude when I popped it on the board.

I have struggled with my weight for as long as I can remember. When I was in dance class as a kid, I was obsessed with staring at the other girl's thighs. I had heavier thighs than most and I compared my thighs to their thighs all the time. I believe I focused on thigh comparison in dance class more than the dance.

I celebrated girls with heavier thighs because it made me feel better about myself. However, in actuality, it was rare. I felt I was always the one in class with the heaviest thighs. If I sat and quantified all of the brain wave energy spent comparing thighs my entire life, I could have probably read hundreds of books and put that wisdom into practice. But no; I was using my precious brain space to compare something 3D—my thighs.

Also when I was very young age, my uncle and aunt made a comment that I was chubby. I doubt they remember saying it, but it stung and took a nice comfy seat in my brain. When I look back, I certainly was not chubby; but again, the comment stuck with me and I remember being judged on my weight as a kid to this day.

I wore teen-sized clothes before the other girls my age because I was taller and a bit bigger. But, again, the crazy thing was that I was not overweight. It was perception based on the norm at the time in the 70's and early 80's. Now, I can't even imagine how much pressure and misery that causes in people, and my heart goes out to anyone who struggles with their weight.

Thinking about the little things that sat in my subconscious, when I didn't truly have the same challenges as others, provides the framework for so much compassion for others. If you are a person who struggles, I am sending you love now.

So, what happened in December of 2020 was eye opening. I saw the notecard and realized I had manifested the weight loss that had happened a few months prior. In June of 2020, a former co-rep told me she was busy coaching on weight loss. I asked her briefly about it, she said she had lost 38 pounds and was super happy. I said, "Sign me up!"

I didn't think anything more about it. All I knew was, "If she can do it, I can too." Literally, that's it. I didn't overthink it; I didn't need to analyze the program, figure out the money or any other excuse delay that people use because they are not ready to take action. *News flash—Yes, people, those are excuses not just for weight release/loss, but anything you desire to do but are procrastinating.*

I was like, *Let's go!!!* I ended up losing 40 pounds in 3 ½ months. Here's the crazy thing: I never thought I could be this thin. That's why it's so nuts. I let it go. I let go of all the notions, expectations, inner dialogue—I sent it away—far, far away and just focused on feeling good and doing what I needed to do. *Bye Bye!* I didn't stress, worry, or think much about it. I just did it. And it worked.

That's the ticket. We are all supposed to just do the thing and feel good in the process so the Universe can pick up the momentum and take it from there. I visualized myself two pounds lighter every time I hit the scale—just two pounds. And if I had a stall, I was okay with it. I was at peace. I understood that it would all happen, and every day I was doing something towards the progress I wanted to see; i.e., not sitting and eating a tub of Ben & Jerry's.

Little by little, two pounds here, one pound there, and some days the scale moved three pounds. The excess weight fell off, and it's been off ever since. How did this happen? I put it out there and let it go. When it showed up, I took action, let it go again and had fun.

Afterward I had this major life-shifting revelation, which I think was even more fun than the actual weight release. I thought it would be a great idea to create Vision Boards with my nieces when I stayed with them in February. What would they desire at their age? What would come to manifest? Would they even be interested in such an activity?

We worked on the boards when I went to visit in February. I gathered a lot of magazines, even purchased a few, and what was amazing is that they primarily wrote on the white index cards I had brought with me, as well. We shall see what ends up manifesting! Feel free to pass this idea along! Again, if I had known all of these things as a kid, I can't even imagine where I would be now as an adult.

Now, where is my dream house?

> "I trust the next chapter because I know the author."
> —Unknown.

Chapter 13

Money is Energy

"Happiness is not in the mere possession of money. It lies in the joy of achievement, in the thrill of the creative effort."
—Franklin D. Roosevelt

WE NEED TO HAVE THE money discussion.

And keep this in mind—*Money Is Energy*. I learned this when I was studying Kabbalah and it stuck with me. Kabbalah teaches that money is not really ours, it's the Universe's. We are managing the Creator's money (*Living Kabbalah* by Yehuda Berg. Kabbalah Publishing).

Once you shift your mindset around money, you are never the same.

Let's start this super important chapter with the positive...

I am constantly amazed, and might I add a bit envious in a celebratory way, of all the manifestation experts that have made a lot of money (some millions) from teaching others tools and tips to manifest money. When you dig back and study those people's successes, it often came out of being dirt poor, living on someone's couch, in debt, filing bankruptcy, etc., which makes me love and celebrate them even more. I often feel that they don't share the back story enough. Maybe it's because they think others will not view them as credible? In my opinion, it's the opposite. I love to hear how they worked through their money challenges and arrived at the thriving place of where they are now.

On the flip side, manifestation coaches often make it seem as if their millionaire success happened overnight. That makes me crazy! Because, unless something supernatural happens or the timing of your energy along with what you may have been unknowingly manifesting happens, it can take years of mindset work, busting through limiting beliefs, understand the principles of The Law of Attraction, and Universal alignment. Oh! And don't forget taking action and building compounding momentum—yes, actually doing something to make money.

Since the expert's journey isn't often shared, the average person may give up, become frustrated, or keep spending money on "the next big thing/person" because they are not doing the work they have already learned nor realizing that it may take time.

It's the shiny object and FOMO (Fear of Missing Out) syndrome which can overcome someone on their road to riches. And believe me, I have been there too.

What's the next nugget or word of wisdom? Have I missed any detail?

I have learned to look at money wisdom (and manifestation) from several angles, which I will share with you in hopes that you see yourself or pick up a new perspective that levels up your journey.

- Working on your limiting beliefs. *I have heard that so many times; really, Melinda?*

- Understanding that money comes back to you. Don't stress about it.
- None of us really become destitute. Money always appears if you let go and believe.

You are okay!

Now, the negative examples...

Well, what some folks may consider being negative.

I strongly feel this piece needs to be written because it can be relevant in the spiritual coaching space and isn't often discussed.

Why don't more spiritual teachers embrace money or have positive money mindsets?

To this day, money mindset continues to baffle me. Others' lack of a positive money mindset has affected some of my relationships with spiritual teachers whom I love and admire. It saddens me, but I have had to either part ways with or love them from a distance.

I know...

- Money is energy
- The world is abundant
- You are worthy

Can you say those affirmations and believe them? Feel them? Many spiritual teachers cannot. They feel bad charging for their services. They judge others who earn a nice living, even if they themselves have become wealthy or millionaires. Even worse, they penny-pinch. I have seen it with my own eyes, and I have been judged for desiring success.

Luckily, it didn't affect me; I saw it as *their* limiting belief. I have done work on myself recognizing where my desire stems from and how others behave as a mirror. To me, the more money I have, the more generous I can be. I LOVE being generous. Being generous lights me up and is my soul purpose (readings with Debbra Lupien). It is not from ego, as others would judge. Their judgment is on them and a state of lack or from their own mistakes.

I have always been generous, and this will not change. So, the more I have, the more I can give. How can that be evil? But, I was portrayed as evil. Truth. And I am no longer friends with those spiritual teachers. Sad but true. I had to walk away from their energy; it did not serve me and certainly won't serve them.

I remember hearing from Tony Robbins that if you were generous before you were wealthy, you become more generous when you become wealthy and vice versa. I believe this to be true because I have witnessed it many times over.

I am giving these examples with love, and if you happen to be that person whose example I am using, it's only meant to shed light and maybe help someone else. Names have been changed to protect the person because, again, it's done with love.

This section may trigger you. If it does, please do the work. Triggers are meant to help you evolve. We are all worthy of abundance—again, money is energy. Even if you gave it all away to charity, imagine how that would help others. Why not desire abundance and stop shaming others and/or limiting yourself?

If you have witnessed someone with a lack mindset, revert to the saying, "See Yourself as Others" so you can move past it with grace.

Your Time is Up

Years ago, I had a reading with a spiritual teacher. We agreed on the price, which was more than fair. When the agreed-upon time was up, we were just getting started and there was so much more to unpack. To me, the price was low, especially for what she was uncovering. It was miraculous what she was saying; life changing. Price should never be an issue in transformation. However, she abruptly stopped the reading, saying, "Your time is up."

Of course, I wanted to go forward! And we did. It struck me that it was like she had the timer set. I have had many readings before and yes, they are timed and I understand that, but sometimes they go over or the vibe to continue is more casual. Her vibe was very money-driven; from a space of lack. I ended up paying her more for karma, gratitude and to maybe seeing it wasn't about the money.

$5 is $5

If you follow me, you know I love to promote people's businesses. This particular reader was offering a special for my audience. The special was $125 for an hour reading. A great price! I made the error of promoting the reading as $120 for an hour. An honest mistake which I didn't even catch, nor would I have, except for what she told me. Telling me is fine, no big deal; however, the vibe was so off in that she was "going to allow it for this instance." Hmm…$5? I could understand the vibe with a larger amount—totally get it. But $5? $5 is money people easily pay for one fancy latte at Starbucks and some folks drink several of those a day. $5 to me in my money mindset is small. I can easily get back $5. A larger amount may be harder to reacquire. But $5? Really? I apologized, understood her mindset, and moved on.

It's Okay to Want Nice Things

The following example is a bit more painful. I have to say, though, that when you have done the work, which took me years, it's easier to understand where other people's beliefs stem from and to stand tall in your power.

Some people can do this; some cannot. Some don't understand and may fall victim to someone else's belief systems. One of the most popular spiritual teachers is Abraham Hicks. Abraham always speaks positively about money and desire. Abundance is consistently infused into their teachings.

Do you love to throw parties? Going all out on good food, fun beverages, even decorations to host a fun and memorable party? Think back to some of the best parties you have been to. What do you remember? What made you smile?

Seeing people's faces lit up and enjoying their surroundings is a beautiful experience. The Law of Attraction also works in this regard. Feeling good and liking nice things brings more nice things into your life. The basic principle I am sure you know, but let's face reality; people forget.

A few years ago, my good friend Richmond suggested having a launch event for my coaching and speaking business. I jumped at it; what a great idea! Not even realizing I was a Human Design Generator, I was super excited and my head started whirling around all of the ideas and possibilities.

However, I didn't think I could hold court on my own and thought it would be fun to collaborate with some other spiritual teachers who could be speakers. Again, I love to collaborate and include others. It's my nature, and I thrive on it.

With the perfect people in mind, jazzed at the mix of gifts we each had, I thought that this was going to be fun!

I am a planner by nature and am 100%+ grateful for this gift. However, I am more than happy also to delegate and gather ideas, as I used to manage large teams and learned to adjust my behavior many years ago. Hearing others' ideas and giving credit to them is fun!

I should have known better when I mentioned the event and feedback from both of the other people was, "Yes that sounds great, but I have no money." To me, it wasn't about the money at all. If they could contribute something, fabulous, because again money is energy and I had planned to pick up the tab and consider it a gift I was thrilled to give to them.

We met in person to preplan. Both of the other women chose to take care of a specific planning task. One woman was to create the marketing flyers, the other was to work on the beverages. Both did not do what they said they would do and asked me to take it on. Fine. Red flag again, but I moved forward.

Excitement was building for the event! All the details were working out perfectly and I was thrilled that so many aspects were either being donated or offered at a discount. The nice bamboo chairs for the guests were surprisingly inexpensive. A friend I met at an Abraham Hicks event donated her time to come and video record the event. The professional photographer's price was extremely fair, if not underpriced. The DJ was volunteering, and we were also not being charged for the property. The bartender had created fun cocktails and was donating her time to serve, assuming she would get tips. So many great things were manifesting perfectly, and I was so grateful.

We charged $25 per person, which also included alcoholic and non-alchoholic beverages. I admit, I felt strongly about that because drinking in The Keys is very common and I felt that based on my experience, some type of alcoholic beverage would be expected. The ticket cost was meant to cover some of the expenses, and we were unaware of what kind of turnout we would have. I was very clear that I would pick up the balance. It was my first time holding an event like this, and "You don't know until you go." *Sorry, popular fishing expression.*

The day of the event had arrived, and my excitement was over the moon! I had been practicing my talk for what seemed like months.

As the day went on, I got very nervous and into my head. My human brain started thinking of all the things that could go wrong. Vicious mind loops got the best of me. It was becoming painful. There was a point of extreme anxiety, and at one point I got very dizzy and almost passed out! I was so deep in my head with self-created fear that I considered canceling. *I can't do this! What was I thinking? Am I nuts? Should I cancel?*

Luckily, since I had started meditating, I quickly reached into my tool bag, started deep breathing and prayed to the Archangels, "Please help me get through this." I also whipped out my journal and started writing...

Within less than 10 minutes, my anxiety subsided, and I was fine. Amazing. If you don't have this as a practice, try it. No, DO it!

The event was perfect! Was I the best speaker? *Um...no...um...* No, lots of um's—it was great to have the video to watch and learn. We had an incredible turnout for a first-time event where none of us had a huge following, or any following at all. I basked in gratitude for everyone's contribution and a sense of accomplishment for putting together something nicely done with an overall great vibe. You must be wondering, "What could go wrong from there?"

I am the first to admit that I am not a financial planner or wiz in general with finances. However, I can keep track of basic expenses on a spreadsheet. Not rocket science, so no need for applause. I also feel in my soul that if someone does something nice for you, i.e., donates their time or helps with promotion, the generous thing to do is to say thank you and, since money is energy, a thoughtful gift card is an excellent way to express gratitude. Anyone else with me?

My two fellow speakers immediately told me they would love to do another event. Fabulous, how fun! I was already visualizing the event growing and helping more people, and that the word would spread. However, if we were to go down this path, it was fair for me to show the expenses, so they were aware of what things cost as I was not going to pick up the tab for the next round. We needed to figure it out, i.e. charge more for tickets, increase the number of guests and advertise, get sponsors, etc.

So, I shared the spreadsheet. To say that email didn't land well... you would have thought I ate their favorite cupcake. *Best analogy I could think of as I am reliving this not so fun experience—and if you ate my favorite cupcake, I would definitely be pissed off!*

Shame on me, I should have better used my intuition. Truly, hand on heart, my mistake. If you are intuitive, you have to learn to follow your intuition. As with anything, everything is a lesson. This is one example. I should have heeded the red flags about the money comments which were made throughout the planning experience. I was definitely sensing money mindset differences.

The mindset was so clear from the one speaker on the day of and what she said in her talk about not making money in her chosen career. Something I have come to realize time and time again is the need to pay attention! Get off my little path and realize I am not the only one in the picture. To say they were not pleased with being shown expenses was the understatement of the year. In fact, it highly triggered them, which led to a scheduled meeting to recap the event. I was braced for this. Above and beyond braced, for which I am forever grateful to my high intuition. I had run the scenario by my husband, and he was like, "Oh goodness, this is not going to go well." And he was right. I thought, *well maybe since they both got clients from the event they will start to see how this can help people and be a good business opportunity.*

Boy was I wrong!

The scheduled recap at a chain restaurant was a three-hour long disaster, which led to the one of the speakers, who had the most lack mindset, storming out of the restaurant in a huff.

I inquired what the issue was. I paid for the event and I wasn't asking for money. However, as business people, we all needed to recap and be aware for next time (which obviously was not going to happen).

And the response was this:

- People should have brought their own chairs.
- No alcoholic beverages. Alcohol is "spirits."
- They would have had a friend take photos.

I will not feel bad for wanting to do nice things or have nice things. I stand in my power.

I heard a saying years ago that stuck with me and was brought to my mind sitting in that chain restaurant feeling bad for the patient server because we were there so long:

"If we were meant to have a business partner, God would have one."

This quote rang true for me at this moment.

I gave the server a huge tip that night and released the energy. I knew where it was coming from and felt proud that I had worked through my money mindset issues and knew someday I could help someone else with the story.

Don't get me wrong, I went back and forth analyzing the situation. Could I have handled it better? Heck yeah! I should have followed my intuition and read the signs.

Other than that, I needed to be at peace and let it go.

> "You cannot change the people around you, but you can change the people you choose to be around."
> —Unknown

Chapter 14

Every day, I am Learning

Gosh, could there be anything more true than that?

Some days, I feel like saying, *"Okay, am I done learning yet?"*

When I started writing this book, I had an outline. The outline then became a page of scribbles, as I kept jotting down one thing after another. I had a boss years ago when I was a merchant for Victoria's Secret who used to say, "pencils down." That saying is brilliant! And in that 10+ hour day environment, it was welcome! I never forgot it.

But, even though I may be screaming (or crying) inside, learning every day is a good thing.

My massive learning and connecting the dots started with my podcast, The Good Karma Success Coach. It became a networking collaboration tool that I enjoyed. Initially, the podcast was meant for me to share and learn how to be a better speaker.

Believe it or not, I started the podcast without a social media presence. Most people build a social media following, then start a podcast.

Nope, not me; I had to do it the hard way and start one without a following. When I think back, it's incredible that anyone found me and listened. I started Instagram and Facebook around the same time, but was hiding and not posting very often.

I made my Facebook page public in February 2021. Crazy, huh? I am definitely not a follower of all the expert advice that's available. As Deb Frueh told me in my first tarot card reading with her, "You seem to take the hard road." Yep, she was right.

Why is that? I scratch my head a lot on this one. I don't mean to. It's not my desire to take the long road.

Why, why, why?

Sometimes it's maddening. I have felt stuck in my life more times than I could ever count. I think of all the things I have been through; being stuck is one of the worst feelings. I know that sounds terrible and selfish, because obviously death isn't a pleasant experience. But I could not control any of the loved ones in my life dying. Being stuck is something I feel I should have control over and don't. Hence the madness.

Every time I have had major stuckness…it has resulted in a breakdown. Tears flowing, screaming, asking for help breakdown. I recall having a breakdown on my blue couch in May 2018, but it shifted and I had some aha moments.

My higher-self says, "It's my lesson so I can help others."

Why do we rush the journey? I have heard many times from many sources, "Growth and evolution over a lifetime." I get it. But the generator Aries in me gets a little annoyed.

I had a major awakening in January that shed so much light on this matter. I started meditating two to three times a day, really working on clearing my energy. My mind became very clear and less crowded with crap. It was an amazing experience. Things would just come to me. *Pop on in!* I have always been creative, but became even more so. And in addition to creativity, the amount of aha moments were becoming quite the daily occurrence. I even referred to one experience in CMFC with the Ace of Swords in Chapter 13.

In early 2021, I had discovered an online marketing business coach. He was offering a Q1 Coaching Bundle. I did not think twice about signing up for the January section. It called to me. But I was struggling with making a decision about the remainder of the package. Over and over, for weeks I labored, *Should I buy it? Do I need it? What was holding me back? Money? Time?* And most importantly, over and over in my head, I would ask myself, *would I be missing some major key to success?*

I know this is what keeps us all in this learning pattern. And it's okay, I guess, if you use the information. But many people don't. Again, circling back to the Intro where I ask Debbra Lupien if it's bad that I have had so many readings. I do use the information, but there is still a point where I have to trust myself.

My mind-opening revelation was realizing that any triggers that I was experiencing towards the courses were my frustration with the fact that I was not comfortable with my marketing.

I was struggling with the reason to buy because none of those were actual reasons to buy or not buy. It was my issue. The inner voice had nothing to do with anyone or anything but me. I have to say, once I realized the source of that voice, a massive wave of relief came over me.

I couldn't do anything different than what I was doing at that moment. I couldn't change time. I couldn't reverse it. I had to become settled in the proud feeling I had of all the real-life experiences I had offline. In comparison, I had more to offer than I was giving myself credit for.

That's what people do when they compare. They knock themselves down instead of realizing what their gifts, talents, and experiences can offer and celebrate them. That day shifted my awareness forward in an incredible way. And yes, I went back to my computer and purchased the rest of the Q1 Bundle.

But…here is more learning. And mind you, as I tell this story, none of it is wrong or negative, it's just to share the journey as yes, it's been a journey and I am sure there are other people in a similar spot.

So, I started the courses. The thing about any coaching—whether it be online through a course or a Facebook Live situation—is that you cannot control the content. Private coaching, yes; except I have had a bad coach before. More on that another time.

So, you may start taking a course and it may not be what you expected or need. It happens. Again, nothing wrong with that. I can always take something away from any course, such as validation of a thought process or methodology, an idea on how to market your services through modeling them, or a reminder of something you forgot or maybe were not doing. The course may provide absolutely nothing new to you (that would be very rare), but you can always learn something.

The trick of this is knowing when you have bought enough courses and start using your intuition to guide you. That was my further learning. Stop consuming so much content. It's hard when you wish to keep learning and growing, but your soul and spirit team are telling you to start being more quiet and let your own thoughts come through. That is the stage I was in. The content was great, but for me it was just validating thoughts and ideas I already had, which then made me feel yucky, like I was copying his content, and I wasn't copying at all.

Did I need to buy it? Likely not on a surface level, but deep down I needed to experience this transition myself. I needed to learn that I had it all within me and it was time to roll with it. Sometimes those lessons are painful and hit the pocketbook, but if it helps to learn it that way, it is worth it.

Fast forward a few months, and here we go again. I start listening to someone else's content, and she has a program. I bought some smaller courses and picked up some minor tweaks here and there about better ways to say things that I already thought and was practicing; a little mindset shift back into alignment and some validation. All well worth the amount spent and the time. But then, she announced her big annual package. It wasn't cheap, but had ton of value. So, my mind started on its creeper course, taunting…

"Do I need this?"

"Will I be missing some magical element to my business if I pass?"

Oh no, what's wrong with me? Haven't I learned my lesson? I even had a reading with Margo Parks the day of this unraveling, which told me several times that I had enough content, "You are good!"

But still, that ego-centered mind with a lack of self-esteem crept up on me again. And here's the thing; just like the other course package I mentioned, I had no feelings towards it. I had no desire to jump online and buy it. My feeling was "meh." The annual program was just out there taunting me.

The online coaching packages I had purchased in the past, when I was just getting started, were an instant, "I have to have this!" My whole body was into it. This was not the case now.

I should have taken the sign and rolled on.

But no, here's what happened. The next morning, bright and early (well, not bright, as it was dark out), I left for my 5 a.m. walk. At the farthest point, which is the street I desire to live on someday, the creeper was doing fine work in my conscious brain.

I stopped and asked, "Is this a test?"

And my whole body lit up like a Christmas tree. On fire! No joke!

There was my answer, it was a test. A test to see if I knew that I didn't need the content. Nothing negative about the coach or her program. But I have come so far in my personal and spiritual journey, it was time to move on from the content.

It Is Done.

Chapter 15

Celebration and Gratitude

> "Celebration is a party in the name of gratitude."
> —Melanie Ann Layer

The Money Happy Dance

I FEEL CALLED TO SHARE this easy, fun tool. If you already practice the money happy dance, high five!

I have gotten to the stage in my life where I don't care much what others may think. I have mentally gotten to a place of chalking it up as, "I bet they wish they could do the money happy dance in the parking lot."

Do you find money when you are out and about? Loose coins? And if so, do you celebrate it?

I find coins often. Do you? It's not every day, but in some cases once or even twice a day. Yesterday I found both a nickel and a dime.

The day before, I found a shiny new quarter. And the day before that was a penny.

I remember being in the checkout line at our local Winn Dixie grocery store. A lady in front of me, who looked to be in bad health, dropped some change on the ground. She walked away and left it. The whole scene happened quickly, and then she was gone, so I didn't feel bad picking them up. If you think about this situation and how she left the coins, I wonder how this works with the Universe?

When I find money, I celebrate. Yes, often I even do a little dance.

I found a dime in the parking lot when I went to the hardware store with my husband. I danced outside of our car. Ryan wanted to hide. His famous saying when he's embarrassed by me is, "Please help me!" Too bad. I did my dance.

> "Dance like nobody's watching."
> —Mark Twain.

(See, even Mark Twain danced around when he found money!)

One day when I was up on the mainland running some errands, I was outside some stores in a strip mall area and happened to look down and see some pennies on the pavement. My excitement grew about finding the lucky pennies and as I stopped to pick them up, I realized that there was a young lady close to me.

Oops! I don't want to be snagging her lucky pennies too.

So, I stopped and asked her if she wanted any of the pennies. She looked at me a bit stunned but very politely and said, "No, but my grandma used to do that, too." She was likely laughing at me especially because I was so excited! But in my head, I was like, *Smart grandma.*

I started putting the change I have found in a pretty Beatriz Ball handmade heart dish and keep it on my desk for Good Karma. That feels good!

I even feel that a red cardinal or the hummingbird that comes to visit is a sign from my guides. Someday I will be thrilled when a White Egret appears in my backyard. At this moment, we don't live on the water so it would be odd; therefore a definite sign. I tested the Universe years ago asking for a hummingbird when it wasn't quite yet hummingbird season. The next day, the first one of the season appeared. Magic!

What signs do you see? Do you celebrate them? Or do you just keep on going?

I have been guilty of "keep on going" over the years, but now I am more intentional with celebrating. I know I was driving my husband, Ryan, bat shit crazy for a while, but he eventually decided to laugh and play along.

If you remember our money story from *Confidence Mastery for Couples*, the Universe doesn't know if you are playing or not making it extremely important to be intentional with what you say and how you act.

I have always felt the celebration of small moments of joy. I started celebrating my podcast listens back in the fall. For the most part, it's worked, and I have had some great podcast months with more listens. *Do I need to celebrate even more?*

I first heard of Melanie Ann Layer at the end of March, 2021. She is an online spiritual coach who has done extremely well for herself. She often shares that one of her main keys to success is celebrating and checking in on your feelings throughout the day.

Seems simple, right? This is the part I always feel I talk about—it seems simple but not always easy. Hearing thoughts from her, especially at her level of success, validated my current practice and affirmation to ramp it up! I have been celebrating things for years, but now it's even more intentional. *Go big or go home!*

Our human brain rules our day, and we run on autopilot. So remembering to do this is what's important.

- Be aware
- Stop
- Do

You could easily pick up the penny you found on the street and pocket it. You could exhibit zero energy about what you found and keep on moving along.

But the bigger step is raising your vibration (aka energy), then dancing around for a minute and saying "thank you" a few times.

That's the work. That's the hard part.

Celebration is an essential part of manifesting and The Law of Attraction. Sure, I say thank you for gifts. I also layer gratitude in our evening prayers and meditations. But, I also have been giving gratitude to even smaller things like Facebook post comments or my plants looking healthy. Stop and think about the additional things you can appreciate and level up your gratitude.

It's common for most adults to live on autopilot. Reflect on your day. Was a majority of your day on autopilot?

Another aspect of Human Design that I tossed into my blender of realization is that being a Generator and primarily left-brained, the action part of me doesn't take a moment to stop, become aware, and celebrate. *Who am I kidding? Sometimes I feel like I even forget to breathe!*

As I mentioned earlier, I tended to be the "keep on going" type. I have worked hard to change my pattern, but I am still not perfect. It takes a lot of awareness (work!) to change those patterns ingrained from an early age. When I think back to my dad always saying, "work hard," it starts there. He didn't say, "Take a moment to smell the flowers."

The work we do as adults to untrain our brain and become more balanced is crucial to our personal development and ability to grow.

Check In on Your Celebration Mindset

I have a friend, Candace, who is an independent sales rep, which means she works for herself on commission. She lives in the Mid-Atlantic area and has on-and-off struggles with the company she works with and how they are particular about selling other lines.

Life & Love Lessons

These parameters are unfair company practices that happen on occasion. If you are not good at standing up for yourself, let alone the fact that legally you are allowed to do whatever it takes to earn income, i.e. selling more products, this mindset can stifle you. I digress.

Anyhow, so in her struggles and trying to figure out a way to move forward, it came to me to connect her with another sales rep that I know, Beth, who ventured out and started her own sales company. Both of these women are very nice, so I figured they would get along fabulously. And they did.

A few weeks went by and I was catching up with Candace, and she was telling me how it had been going so far. The conversation was primarily about her concerns. Her concerns were that now she had too many products to sell, had to travel more, and she was afraid to post on social media.

I thought she would have had excitement, celebration, and gratitude for a possible way out of the other situation. I was excited for her and shared some of the positive aspects but, it didn't seem to elevate her mood. She kept bringing up the potential challenges. Furthermore, this new company was an incredible opportunity to increase her income. The whole experience was a bummer and I had to move on from the conversation.

Where was her celebration and gratitude for her own potential?

Mindset

If you don't have a mindset for celebration and gratitude, will the Universe keep rewarding you? Or even a heart-centered soul in a human body, such as myself? Most people may say, "Phooey on you, next time I am not hooking you up with an opportunity." My grandma used to say phooey. *Love ya grandma! She must be hanging with me now for me to think of that word.*

So much more can go into the practice of celebration. I can celebrate my flowers blooming, a butterfly in my window view, our dogs not barking in the middle of the night, the sunrise on my morning walks, or just things going my way for the day. The more you practice it, the more life tends to unfold for you with possible blessings. When I hear stories from people about things never going right for them, I often wonder if it's because they are not practicing celebration and gratitude. It is amazing how some people's lives tend to work out where they don't have little things happen, or if something big is transpiring, it ends up for the best. Technically, everything ends up for the best, but it's the way you look at it.

Again, mindset.

Tip: Find some way to remind yourself to check in on gratitude and celebration until it's a fundamental practice.

Ideas to help remind yourself to stop, check in, and be grateful or celebrate:

- Set the alarm on your phone.
- Put a sticky note somewhere you will see it often, like on your desk or in your car.
- Use an activity—such as every time you take a sip of water.

It just takes small moments throughout the day to retrain your brain. And once you retrain your brain, it will be a basic activity in your life and you can watch the miracles flow.

Thank you for the large white feather that floated down from the sky in front of my office window. I don't see a bird, so I assume it came from my angels…Thank you!

> "Feathers are reminders that angels are always near."
> —Unknown

Chapter 16
Sending Good Thoughts

"Focus on the positive things in your life and you'll be shocked at how many more positive things start happening."
—Sophia Amoruso

YEARS AGO, I READ A book by Sophia Amoruso called *#Girlboss*. I remember her saying to make your passwords something inspirational or an affirmation. Something of that sort; don't quote me on exactly how she said it, it's been a while.

But the gist is that we all use passwords so much *(understatement, right?), so* why not make your passwords an affirmation so you're putting your desires out there to the Universe? I thought that was an awesome idea and one I had not heard before. *Now I need to go back and read that book again...I may find something else I missed.*

My affirmation passwords are pretty lofty, so they haven't happened yet. As Debbra Lupien heard from my guides on one of her monthly Ask Your Guides zoom calls, "I have a big recipe." *Yep! So, check back with me in a few years.*

Ryan's are pretty close to manifestation and a little more general. I manage his passwords for our checking account, too, so my manifesting wizardry is in the works for him.

Maybe I should bring mine down a notch? Nah...dream big!

Note—This chapter segues into energy and celebration, which are covered in other chapters as well. But, as I mentioned in the beginning, so many of these shifts work together and I felt like making this its own chapter.

Candles are a Trigger?

Like most people being stuck in the pandemic, in the Fall of 2020, I had some big Aha moments. I realized, I had icky feelings towards a lot of things. It's embarrassing but true. I had icky anxiety whenever I would receive an email asking me for something regarding a candle company I repped.

I already mentioned I had not-so-happy feelings about saying "super excited" in my podcast and my Good Karma Success Coach branding. I recognized these feelings more and more. And I needed to make some changes fast!

The email trigger was an eye-opener. Recognizing and understanding where it stemmed from was critical in order to crush it. *Squash it like a bug.*

Triggers can be damaging, but believe it or not, they are meant to help you. The majority of people do not like talking about triggers, let alone recognizing them. But it's crucial.

I beg you, move past your shame or embarrassment and work on them, pronto!

Life & Love Lessons

The email trigger happened was when I was a sales rep for a large and very popular candle line. I used to receive countless emails about minor issues such as:

- "Where is my invoice?"
- "This candle is broken."
- "Where is my shipment?"

All of these were issues for which the company was notorious for having challenges. A lot of short shipments, late shipments, missing invoices, broken candles, etc. My whole day could be sucked up dealing with what are called "claims." It was annoying and grated on my nerves every day all day long.

The constant claims created a block in which I started to have anxiety around emails.

How did this end up manifesting?

ALL emails became a trigger and made me feel yucky!!!! *Ugh!*

So, for example, when someone signed up for my Good Karma Confidence newsletter, I would receive an email notification.

My head would say, "Oh no! What now?"

And it was someone joining my email list. Geez. A happy thing turned icky because of the candle emails.

Yikes! I started to realize what was going on and quickly shifted to celebration.

Now, when I see the alert, I am super happy and excited, "Yay! Someone signed up—thank you!"

We also celebrate when my husband sells an online course. It's a brief, happy thank you and then we roll on with our day.

This can happen for so many people on many levels. I know it can happen with coaching calls. I would bet this happens more often than not, or than anyone wants to admit.

The fear, anxiety triggers and mind loops may sound something like this:

- "Can I really do this?"
- "Who am I?"
- "Will this be a lot of work?"

And perhaps some other mind loops get triggered.

I also had an instance that I wasn't aware of until the day it was going to take place. I had an icky feeling around a mini-course I was launching, and had been happily promoting.

What? Seriously, I couldn't believe it.

I had been sending the mini-course all the good vibes for weeks, doing all the things the experts teach in marketing and promotion.

But on the day of the launch, during my morning walk, I realized my chest was frozen. That's how I tend to feel wrongness, "Is my chest tight?" That's the best way I can explain it.

So I used deep breathing and talking myself through it. "I give myself permission" is a great tool, as I mentioned in the previous chapter. Also, journaling can help relieve the tension. It was too late to save the mini course, which I ended up canceling, but it was a great lesson for next time.

If you have any of this happen, think of it like a muscle in that you may not have the kink or cramp worked out right away, but if you can work at these things it will loosen up.

Triggers, Mind Loops, and Energy

Call me crazy, but I love to talk about triggers. The fascination and excitement are in direct correlation to my love of energy. I am always perfecting my energy. It's my mission.

When I looked up triggers on-line, the definition is very trauma based. So I will share from my perspective as it's not just for trauma experiences.

Triggers are an internal warning system meant to shed awareness on something. It can be something someone says, does, or even how they look. It can also be situational and not necessarily a result of another person. When you experience a trigger, you receive an internal feeling that doesn't feel good. I would compare the feeling to mild anxiety. It is taught that triggers are meant to help you move through a past challenge, trauma, or general feeling so you can feel more joy. I would agree with that. Once I started to recognize and move through my triggers, I felt more at peace and more joy.

I would dare to say we all have triggers and mind loops at some point. Mind loops are when you continue to repeat a past situation or conversation over and over in your head. You cannot escape it and it can be maddening or at the least frustrating. Mind loops consume energy that is better spent on something positive and productive. Some people are better at moving through them. They may have had to learn how to move through them, or if they are super lucky, maybe they are wired this way.

I would also venture to say that some people may not really notice stuff as much as others. It could be that their soul isn't as old, perhaps? Or how they are wired? Who really knows, right? We can theorize and ask our guides, but we cannot really control it.

And some people jump to reaction mode when they are triggered and can cause physical or psychological harm. Those reactions are nothing to joke about.

When you bust your triggers, you have a breakthrough and your life and mental state lightens step by step. It's a unique process. I have had many to bust through, too many to count, and maybe I could write a whole book on them! Ryan has had a lot of triggers to move through, too—lots and lots. It feels good when you can relax and openly talk about them.

So, here is a big story to share that may surprise you.

My first book, *Confidence Mastery for Couples (CMFC)*, was a trigger. The first time you are a solo author, you have no idea how many pages your book may turn out to be. Fellow authors, bloggers, editors, publishers, etc., all talk in word count.

You will see on social media,

- "I wrote 10,000 words today!"
- "I start my day first by writing 800 words!"
- "Every day, I write a 500-word blog."

I think you get my drift.

Words, words, words.

Even the writing course I had joined in the late fall of 2020 talked about word count, and the coach was a published author with almost 20 books!

The page count was mentioned regarding wanting to have at least 100 pages so your book would have a spine for the title. But, the page count, in relation to word count, wasn't taught.

Coaching YouTube videos also mainly talk about word count and that your book should be at least 100 pages.

In our writing class, the word count which was discussed was a goal of 20-30K words.

How many words did CMFC end up at?

28,000 words. I was celebrating! I was personally goaling at the 25,000 and told my editor, Valerie, it wouldn't be more than 30,000, and it landed at 28,000.

Again, I was celebrating. I was super proud of myself and couldn't believe I naturally hit the target. Talk about The Law of Attraction and manifesting! Woo hoo!

I am not a wordy person. I like shorter, "to the point" facts, tips, stories, and ideas. My ADD-like short attention span kicks in if someone drones on and on.

My attention span deficit kicks in on social media, zoom, in a course, or with a book. It doesn't matter where; I have a short attention span and great respect for time.

Even Ryan gets told to speed it up or "make it tight" sometimes. *Sorry, my love!*

As a Gen X-er, we didn't have ADD back then as a common diagnosis. But it's likely I would have been on the spectrum for how many times I was sent to the principal's office for not paying attention. I digress.

So, what happened? I got my book in my hands and was like, "Wow, it's kinda thin, and only 116 pages? Geez, I just made the cut."

And it brought my energy and high vibes down.

I kept it very quiet, inside my head, but every time I looked at my paperback copy, I felt a little sad.

Then I realized my book size was a trigger. The trigger appeared when someone wrote her review for my book and called it an "easy, quick read."

Ouch! She meant no harm at all, and she had no idea what was going on in my head.

She sent the review to me ahead of posting on Amazon, so I could use it for social media. I said, "Thank you." and never said a word about the comment.

But it sat with me. It stung and festered.

I had to get my shit together around this trigger fast. My book launch was less than a week away and I believe in positive energy and sending good vibes towards all things and people.

I was very proud of my book and I did not want to have sad feelings about it. I loved it! To start to feel sad about something so stupid, such as page count, was utterly ridiculous.

I needed to block out all the social media bullshit noise where other authors bragged about their page count. I needed to have a real "come to you know who" about my content, its value, and my purpose.

Those are things I knew intuitively, but this darn human brain was just overriding my love to help others and the matter in which I communicated the message.

What to do…

How could I shift my mindset and energy?

Hmm…well I have a ton of books; let's take a deep dive and see who we find.

It was as if Robert Greene and Richard Dotts came over for tea and biscuits.

Do you know who Robert Greene and Richard Dotts are?

They are both extremely successful authors. Both of whom I have several of their books on my bookshelf. And I also have Robert Greene on Audible.

If you know who they both are—kudos, and maybe you will guess where I am going with this comparison.

If not, here's the scoop:

Robert Greene's books are very long! *Mastery* is 336 pages, and *The Laws of Human Nature* is almost 600 pages. *Mastery* on Audible is 16 hours! No shit! And there are many summary books out there for his titles. If another author can capitalize off of summarizing your book, it may be that it's long, right?

Richard Dotts books on average are 103 pages. I counted on my bookshelf; I have eight of his books. I think that's all of them.

Robert's books take him years to write; they are loaded with historical stories to validate his human nature conclusions.

Ricard Dotts is quick and to the point. Each book is focused on one aha moment that is a transformational aspect of The Law of Attraction with some relatable stories.

Again, both very good, and I obviously own them. However, my ADD doesn't allow much Robert Greene in my life. I would rather know more about what Robert thinks, and I usually skip all of his hard work in researching historical facts to get to his conclusion, because that's where the meat is. Sorry, Robert.

Now, if I were retired and sitting in a beach house all day, sure, maybe I would have more time to read all that. On second thought, no, not likely. I would still skip to Robert's conclusions and messages.

Here's my mindset shift. I prefer Richard Dotts's books, hands down, to Robert Greene's? Why?

I can read one in a weekend while relaxing in my hot tub under the palm trees.

Which then leads me to feel accomplished after I read them.

They are easy, fun reads, and I don't get stressed out by all of the pages and the mindset of, "I will never finish."

They are not loaded with extra stuff. The extra jargon in general in the publishing world, especially in big name periodicals, is blowing my mind. I would much rather have quick and easy, to the point stories, ideas and tips. Some call it fluff, some call it jargon. Whatever you wish to call it likely suits what it is for you about that particular piece of content. For me, it's a pass.

After I went through this exercise, a ton of weight came off my shoulders. I finally felt at ease and told my human brain and ego in this case to "sit the f down."

I love my book! I am thrilled someone can read it in one weekend, enjoy it, laugh, learn from it and feel accomplished. I value my audience's time as much as my own. The Audible is only three hours long. I have heard great feedback not only about the execution, but also about the length.

The interesting thing that happened was that when the reviewer posted her review to Amazon, she had taken that tidbit about the size out of the review. I about fell over! I never said a word about the trigger. She must have had an intuition hit guide her.

A week or so later, someone else left a review with the title *Easy Read, Big Impact*.

At the end of the day, that was my intention. I felt good about the size and value of the content, and my energy shifted.

Thank you!

Sometimes your human brain just needs some coaching.

Chapter 17

Time and Letting Go

> "Let That Shit Go!"
> —Unknown

I HAVE ALWAYS LOVED THAT saying, so I am using it now for this chapter.

If you could tell me your biggest struggle regarding your thoughts and manifestation, what would that be?

My biggest struggle is time. Hands down, without a doubt, worrying about time and thinking about time.

- *When is it going to happen?*
- *When will things change?*
- *How long will it take* me?

Dang—it kills me! And the crappy thing is that I am aware of it, but my human brain won't listen.

"I am a work in progress."
—Unknown

Do you have the same challenge?

Where does the time mind loop stem from?

My dad made us always be 10 minutes early to everything as children? Not a bad thing, right? So that's a lame excuse. Or is it how we all just get wired from what's around us, i.e. conditioning from society?

Oh, maybe I should let it go on "the why," right?

Geez. Another mind loop. Another layer.

The Ring Experiment

Luckily, I am not someone who tends to lose things. However, I have lost weight, and with the weight loss (I like to say "release" because it's not coming back) I happened to lose a wedding band.

Granted, I have been joking, *well not really joking*, with my husband since early on in our marriage that I will someday get an upgrade. I am not into jewelry like some women, but I would like a nice big ring eventually. Ryan never cares or gets offended, so don't worry about that. I doubt he even understands what I am wearing and what I want. Ryan's a fisherman, remember? If it were about a big wahoo or snapper on my finger, he would likely pay attention, but for a ring, nope.

So, this little joke had been going on for years. AND I have some rings on my vision board.

Pre-Covid-19 I was at a shoe store where I used to sell handbags. The owner of the shoe store, Victoria, is fabulous.

Victoria had this fun faux ring display on her counter, and while she was helping a customer, I was trying on the rings. Of course, I found exactly the ring I wanted as the upgrade! A dazzler! Emerald cut stone that I must say looks amazing on my finger. Yep. It had my name all over it, and Victoria gave it to me.

Tip Share—Always accept gifts!

I was so happy and grateful. I bounced out of her shop, admiring how fabulous this ring looked on me.

Then…I put it away.

Flash forward to April 2021. Six months after my over 40-pound weight release, I was struggling to not only find some new clothes without spending a fortune, but also to keep my rings on my fingers. I was on a group Zoom call when I looked down and noticed I was missing one band.

Oops! Well…maybe an oops? Or perhaps a bigger plan manifesting? *Which way should I look at it?*

I was calm on the Zoom call. "Oh, wow, I lost a wedding band."

I think the rest of the group was a bit struck that I was so calm. I would venture to say that a majority of women would be freaking out and start tearing apart the couch, car, every nook and cranny, and here I was like, "Oh, that's an interesting update."

Intuitively, I realized I had no clue where to start looking, because for all I knew I could have lost it anywhere, even days before, as I don't pay much attention to my rings, and since there were three rings (two bands and the main ring), it didn't feel any different on my finger.

I decided to play a game: Let's see if I don't worry or think about it at all, will the band show up?

Since I already knew that I desired an upgrade, had a fun faux ring to wear in the meantime, and quite frankly, now that this had happened I couldn't wear the rings anymore anyways because they were too big, so I might as well play. Why not? Let's test the Universe and see what happens.

Timestamp:

- Friday: I initially discovered that I was missing the band.
- Saturday: I tried on two different ring replacements, but I settled on the faux emerald cut ring from Victoria.
- Thursday: I found the ring on the bottom of my beach bag.

I found my wedding band in less than one week! You read that correctly!

In less than one week, it magically reappeared. I was at the little local beach for my morning mediation. Afterward I went back to the car and as I moved my wallet from the beach bag back to my everyday tote bag, I saw a small round "something" on the bottom of the bag. I had to pause because it took me a second to even realize what it was...I had obviously put it out of my mind.

But there it was. In all of its non-upgraded, full of love, magicalness. *Is magicalness a word?*

I rejoiced that my experiment worked! Pop the champagne!

Now, what's next? Can I lose my couch that's starting to get a bit worn and a new one will pop into my life? Not a bad idea...

"You may wear out your iron soled shoes searching for what arrives without effort when the time is right."—Chinese Proverb

Valerie

Yes, Valerie, my super incredible editor, is getting a section. *Wonder what she will say when she reads this?*

When I started on the path of writing several books a year, I initially planned to release four books a year. To make this plan work, my second book would need to be turned into the editor by April week one. I made a plan with Valerie in January and she put me on her calendar.

As I moved forward working on the first book, *Confidence Mastery for Couples*, which was released March 9, my timing was coming out a bit different. Best laid plans, right?

As I moved through March, I hadn't gotten as far along on this book as I had hoped and didn't see how I could turn the draft in to her by April 1st. Why? Honestly, things took longer than I had thought in getting CMFC released, and I had more to learn than I realized. So, I swallowed my Type A pride and emailed Valerie for a two-week extension.

Well…wouldn't you know, her world doesn't revolve around me and my schedule. *WTF! So wrong of her. Geez. Just kidding.*

She was nice as can be and here I was jacking up the schedule. But, she wouldn't be able to help me now until Mid-May.

A bit longer than I had thought she would say. I needed to take a pause and regroup.

Not because of anything about her at all. But because my Human Design Generator Action-Oriented Aries brain is wired to be extremely time oriented and it went against my nature to move something out. I had to take a pause and think realistically. Could I realistically write and self-publish four books a year? Or, is three books a year more achievable?

And what did it look like if I let go and relax a bit as I was wrote?

What if?

Would I be able to share even more stories, as my evolution is happening so quickly?

Would my stories have more construct?

What if I didn't think about it and let the Universe take over?

Step one was Valerie's schedule. Step two would be the balance of the process.

Let's take this a step further.

What if we didn't set an official date on the calendar and see what happens?

Wouldn't that be fun?

Well, again, my wired action brain may not see it as fun, so we need to work on that.

But, that's the plan. I am letting go of an exact plan.

And you know what? It wasn't so difficult. I survived, it all worked out and no one else struggled. Maybe the best laid plan isn't a plan?

Part 2

If you follow me on Facebook, you know I have been doing daily Facebook Live events since January, 2021. Going on camera, let alone live, has been a process! A mental challenge on many levels.

As with anything, I am working on improving, I spend some time judging myself. Yes, harshly too, I might add. I also spend time comparing myself to other coaches and their Facebook Lives. I have compared everything from where they shoot their video to how much makeup they have on. Never quite the best feeling. Hence the journey to confidence.

It's virtually impossible, at least for me, to copy someone. The download of content comes to me so quickly that it's challenging to remember all I would like to say. I have tried scripting and it doesn't work for me. I have had to learn through many assessments and guidance that some folks need to be scripted and some don't prefer to be. It's just how they are wired. So, for example, I can always tell that some influencers and online coaches are scripted; they must prefer to be scripted in their human make up.

Where am I going with this?

On Tuesday, April 27, 2021, for a frame of reference, I did a Facebook Live where I tried to be a bit more planful, not scripted but I had a plan for what I was going to share. In that session, two things happened: I forgot to say who I was, and I segued into briefly mentioning the above story about the timeline and letting go. UGH!!! Afterward I had to strongly go against my nature of beating myself up as to not ruin the energy of the video. It was done. And other than those things, for the most part I liked how the session turned out.

I asked Ryan to watch the video and give me his feedback. He liked it a lot because I spoke slower. He struggles with fast talking videos, and especially with how I listen to podcasts on 1.25 speed. Good feedback, as something I have been wanting to do is to slow it down a tad.

The following morning, I went for my walk and listened to Andrea and Truth Well Told Tarot. Her reading for May was extremely on point for me. I felt she was reading just for me. Selfish, I know, but true. I listened to it four times. *I hope it helped her algorithm!*

She intensely spoke about "one more thing" that I needed to clear. Yep, I had heard that before from Margo. One more thing. Seriously. UGH! This "thing" was lingering. *What was that "thing?"*

"Please, guides help me find 'the thing' and solve it!"

I think my guides laughed at me, as I am demanding an answer. Likely, it's a test and I just don't know yet. That dang divine timing, right? *Yep.*

My action-taker brain doesn't like little things lingering that I don't know. It's like finding that damn bug in my house a few days ago and then not being able to catch it. *I finally got it this morning! YES!*

The next stop in my morning "being" ritual was the trip to the little beach. As I grabbed my bag and my chair from the car, I was replaying the Facebook Live from the day before over in my head. I was reliving Ryan's feedback about slowing down, and my hindsight about the Letting Go segue that strayed from my main message. I was beating myself up pretty bad and trying to rationalize it all.

What I came to reckon with was that the Letting Go segue popped out. It literally popped out of my mouth onto Facebook. I didn't control it or pre-think it, which means it was divinely guided.

I needed to stop busting the Universe's ass because…someone out there needed to hear that message.

Chills.

Getting closer to the lesson but not quite yet..still having those pesky human brain moments…

I was lucky that at 11 a.m. that day, it was our monthly Akasha Unleashed Mastermind call led by Debbra Lupien. I knew that during this call, I would have the opportunity to run this whole scenario amongst the group of fellow spiritual intuitives and ask for their advice and guidance.

As I barfed the information, super nervous to suck too much time (and again, I talk fast), I was thrilled at the information that came back to me as confirmation.

Debbra intuitively agreed that I should not be shutting down my channel and to let it flow. What was meant to come out was coming out in the fashion that it was meant to be and was needed. Her insight gave me permission to move on from the mind loop. I needed to move on and stop overthinking and analyzing.

Both Debbra and Laura confirmed my fast-talking was fine and understandable. In general, people are running on tighter timelines now, trying to squeeze more in to their day, so shorter content and at a faster pace is on par. I am on that page, as well.

It was also agreed that I should blog about my ideal, perfect-fit client. Publishing a blog would be good to help me to solidify it with the Universe. I was on that page. I loved the confirmation and validation.

After the call, I breathed a huge sigh and felt so much better. I went to my usual midday meditation and tried to clear my mind.

The message regarding my content came quickly, loud and clear: "It's not about me."

Tears…got it.

April 28, 2021—Healing Energy Tools on Instagram

The Universe is saying to you today:

"Speak your truths. Free yourself from others' expectations, standards, beliefs and opinions.

You don't need anyone's approval to be yourself, only your own."

Collapsing Time

I was doing some research on Alpha Female traits regarding sales as I was working on a podcast. I love YouTube and stumbled upon a YouTube channel that briefly mentioned a book, *Outrageous Openness* by Tosha Silver. Breadcrumbs…

I have to say, I love Tosha's book! I even bought it for my 15-year-old niece, Sienna. I feel that it's one of those fun guidebooks that everyone should have on their table. And I visualize my books to have the same life-changing, thought-provoking effect. *Putting it out there!*

Why do I like this book enough to mention it in my book? Because the stories are easy to read, fast, relatable, and MOST IMPORTANTLY each story gives you the confidence to let shit go!

I do believe, and I am sure others would agree, that if you practice letting it go more and more, let the Universe take the wheel without bad energy or thoughts, have a clear vision, and take inspired action, you will collapse time. Simple? Not for everyone but it's feasible to get there.

Recognizing the above stories and working through the mind loops helps take your hands off the wheel and release it all to the Universe which can then help collapse time.

> "Time is none of your business."
> —Abraham Hicks

And we are all a work in progress.

Chapter 18

Guidance from the Other Side

> "Faith sees the invisible, believes the unbelievable,
> and receives the impossible."
> —Corrie Ten Boom

HAVE YOU EVER HAD A reading from a medium? A really good medium?

"Hey Melinda, how do you know if she/he is a good medium?" you might ask.

Great question! As I am sure it's a bit murky, my gut says that if what the medium says knocks your socks off and completes a journey, that is a good medium. *Bam!* And my reading did just that.

(Please note names have been changed.)

I didn't know this medium, Cathy; she wasn't referred to me, and I hadn't done any research. I just followed my intuition. Even though I had had plenty of tarot card readings before that bordered psychic readings, a reading from a medium (someone who can talk to dead people, and that's the focus) just hadn't happened yet. But I guess it was time, right?

I took a deep breath, said a prayer and began listening.

The reading started with some engagement questions, as someone popped in immediately.

The questions were not quite hitting the mark in conjunction with me going through my database of people I knew who have passed on. Cathy kept digging.

"This woman talks a lot."

Hmm…I rattled off a few people and none of them were correct.

She asked more questions and I responded with more nos.

We weren't getting to the person.

I was scratching my head. I was confused.

I wasn't upset, just trying to rack my brain on whom it was and why was it so hard to think of this person.

The medium, Cathy, kept repeating some of the same traits; talks a lot, loud, describing her appearance. And then finally with one sentence it all clicked, and I said, "That's Joan! But she's still alive."

"Yes, that's her. And if the message you need to hear is what you need to hear. I can pull through a soul even if that person is alive."

Because I do believe in quantum fields, I didn't doubt this at all. It was just something I had never heard before, so I needed to ground myself in the present and then prepare for the message. I also completely believed her because the description was so right on. She nailed it and said things no one would have ever known.

If you are someone who is a not believer, if you had an experience like this, I am quite confident you would shift your mindset. The fact was that she pulled Joan through and the information was above and beyond real and impactful.

After we established who she had pulled, I mentioned, without any reason why, that I did not speak to this person anymore, and it had been many many years. Normally, in the coaching space, I have found that the majority of coaches go down a path of telling someone,

"You need to work it out." "You need to work on yourself." "You need to…." Blah blah fucking blah.

Yep, I said it. No regrets.

Seriously, that's how I feel.

But, as a spiritual being, I do not need to listen to a human who has no idea what my experience is and how I feel. They are just repeating some coaching rhetoric jargon that they heard in class or read somewhere. I am sick of it, and I tend to disconnect myself from those people. The remainder of this story validates my intuition and higher self.

But, in the meantime, because of what's out there, I was braced for some schooling or something…

Instead…

The message from my team of over 30 souls standing behind her was that I did the right thing by walking away.

These were the messages:

"Joan will not change in this lifetime."

"She knows she needs to change and is choosing not to."

"It was good I cut the cords that had been binding."

And finally:

"Everyone was cheering me on."

If you don't get confidence from a reading like that, I don't know what to tell you.

This was life-changing as far as confirming the action I had taken and also my thought process with the coaching industry. My higher-self had guided me and I was glad I listened.

On a super fun note, after that piece, Cathy went on to talk about my husband Ryan and me being on a boat and going really fast. Laughing, dancing, the wind in my hair. And a tall, young, good looking guy spirit was with us.

This one was easy. And again, further validated how amazing she was.

The day before, my husband Ryan and I, on a rare occasion, had taken our boat out for spin in the bay and to see sunset. It's a shame how rarely we do this. Basically, because the boat is our business, and my husband is booked every day, the last thing he wants to do with his downtime is go for a boat ride.

But we did just that the day prior, and we had a blast. We were smiling, laughing and I always play Sirius radio and scroll for the best 80's music.

Cathy had no idea we own a boat, so the vision she was receiving was confusing. Further, when she described the good-looking younger guy who was, might I add, super tall, she had no idea she was describing my brother Bryan, who tragically passed away at 29 years old and was over 6 feet tall.

Crazy good, huh?

When I validated her vision, she also mentioned that he had a big white fluffy dog with him, and they were always together.

Crystal.

Crystal was my parents' dog. She was a gorgeous Samoyed, and my brother adored her. We all did. I could tell Crystal stories all day long. She was a love and since she was a larger dog, it was like she was a person. I will admit, though, that I wasn't a fan of the shedding. *Sorry Crystal!*

When I validated that the dog was indeed a solid message, Cathy further said that Crystal loved her name because of crystals. So cool!

I was able to ask some clarifying questions about my brother's death that had bothered me for years. I had received a thought about how he passed, and then another spiritual teacher had confirmed it. Over time, this thought had bothered me on and off.

It ends up that the thought I had wasn't true. However, my brother was okay with passing on at that time. He said it was his time to go. We all miss him to this day, but obviously he is with us. What a great message and relief to have reckoned with that former thought process. I was delighted!

His message to me was to "focus." Cathy said he was tossing a ball, with the symbolism being to focus on the ball. I had to laugh because, even though I am organized and get stuff done, I tend to have many balls in the air on any one given day, so he was right on. I tend to receive this message from my guides on and off throughout the years, so it's interesting to know that the Universe does want people to focus.

I am still a work in progress. We all are, every day.

Pretty damn good, huh?

Any doubters?

> "When something unbelievable happens,
> you better believe that's God."
> —Steve Harvey

Chapter 19

When am I Going to Listen?

"I have been a seeker and I still am, but I stopped asking the books and the stars. I started listening to the teaching of my soul."
—Rumi

I SAVED THIS CHAPTER FOR last because at the end of the day, in this case book, listening to our higher self is the most important thing we all can do. As Margo Parks told me, "Melinda, you are a spiritual being."

We all are…here we go.

Higher Self

I think my guides have been saying to me, "When are you going to listen?" for years. And I believe I finally have it down. Well, I am not going to say I am perfect by any means, but I finally GET IT.

Yes, it took some hard knocks and some coins, but I am on the right train now.

Are they laughing or shaking their heads?

Listening to your higher self is perhaps one of the most important things you can master. I am going to say that and energy.

Does everyone have it mastered? I doubt it. Maybe like Eckhart Tolle or monks? Not sure, maybe I can invite them to dinner and ask someday. *Putting it out there!*

I didn't quite understand the concept until it started happening at such a rapid pace. And at the same time I was being tested. Yes, tested.

The Walking Test

I hadn't thought of the concept as being a test, but that happens, too. So keep this story in mind if this is new to you.

For me, it happened as I was starting out on my morning walk, when all of a sudden, I had anxiety. My body was tingling all over and I had this feeling that I needed to turn around and go back home. I thought to myself, "This is odd, maybe there is some danger in my path." I was listening to my intuition, but my head was still interrupting. I started my walk along the normal path, which is north. The feeling in my body, a tingling, wouldn't leave. I walked more on the street vs. the sidewalk. The feeling wouldn't leave. I turned around and walked south. The feeling wouldn't leave. I was testing the test.

I turned around again and came home.

The feeling was gone, and I was back to my normal vibe state. Interesting.

I was lucky because I already had a call scheduled with Margo, and immediately told her the story.

"You were being tested to see if you would listen."

Ahhh...I passed.

I get it.

Again, I won't say I am perfect with recognizing my higher self, but I am much better than even the day before, and that's all that counts. And since this test and my understanding, I am spending more time asking, waiting, feeling, and then making a decision.

Here are some examples that may lead you to have some aha moments, as well.

The Importance of Getting Quiet

Today on Clubhouse, the topic of the room was music and connecting with your guides. I like music, but I would never say I am really into music like my best friend and former college roommate Melinda is. Yes, we have the same name, no we are not sisters and yes people ask that. #seriously. Her love and knowledge of music transcends. Sitting here typing this, I just realized that she also manifested her own husband, Scott. And back in 1993 we certainly had no clue what manifestation was. She would clearly say out loud to me that she wanted to marry someone who loved music as much as she did. Scott definitely does. That is so cool that I just got chills!

Okay, back from memory lane…

Refresh…

Today on Clubhouse, I spoke up and shared that I listened to mainly high frequency, meditation music and sound bowls for our dogs. *Yep, sound bowls for our dogs.* All courtesy of YouTube.

I mentioned the above and that I also feel a bit conflicted at times that I don't listen to more music and I was looking forward to hearing others share their stories.

Why do I feel conflicted? I feel there are a lot of influencers and other people on social media who are always talking about music they listen to and I always get this little FOMO feeling when I hear it.

And my brain says:

- "Should I listen to some music?"
- "Am I missing out on something if I don't?"
- "Some big, amazing thing that won't happen until I listen to club music or Beyonce?"

And then I get pulled to do what I normally do, and lately I have been called to have no music at all.

That's the best—silence. Why silence? Because silence helps you clear your thoughts and let other downloads come through from your guides. I am amazingly comfortable in silence. I find it fascinating people always need to have some noise. My sister always has the TV playing country music stations all day. When I watch my nieces, it's silence. I often wonder if my nieces notice or think it's weird. *Hmm…I should ask them.*

So, what happened? The next speaker spoke up about music and how she would listen to songs to elevate her mood. *Bingo! 9.99 times out of 10 I am in a positive high vibe mood, so I don't need music for that. Thank you for the clarity! Challenge solved.*

Send Me a Link

Another instance happened with something that seems to be occurring more and more, and that is people saying, "Send me a link" for something that is easily found online. Could be something in your social media feed or on Amazon.

My first gut response is, "That's lazy." Then my other brain takes over and tries to rationalize the request, "Oh, is it so bad that you have to do that?" or "I should be this really helpful person because they are so busy." WRONG!

Here is where I ended up listening to my higher self. If you cannot take a second to look at my feed and find what we are talking about, you are not in alignment with how I roll. I get stuff done and value my time, too. Bigger than that, I also care about people enough to take some time to find "the thing."

I feel undervalued if you cannot take a second to look for something that is either for you or helpful to me. I believe in the platinum rule to treat others as they wish to be treated, but life is a two-way street.

My time is just as important, and if you want the information just take a second to look for it. Don't dump on me. The interesting thing is that the first person who was doing this "link request scenario," a few times I might add, triggered the memory that she used to dump tire kicker customers on me when I was a new rep and we attended trade shows together. The first trade show I was clueless, as I would never do that to someone.

By the second trade show, I was onto to her and her behavior, and no longer allowed the dumping. I would say, "No, I can't help her as I'm waiting for my appointment." That was the whole gimmick that I picked up on. If you didn't want to help a random customer that you didn't make commission on and was likely a chatty Cathy, you would say, "No, I am waiting for an appointment."

This "send me a link" was a trigger back to her behavior, which made me think back to setting my boundaries and standing up for myself. Hence why it didn't sit well with me. I needed to shut out the noise of what other humans say to do because either they don't mind or they desire you to follow them.

Once I realized this, it became a no-brainer to direct someone to check out my feed or a link in Instagram Bio or just ignore the direction in a Facebook Group message. *Ahhh, that feels good! Thank you, higher self!*

These are two small daily examples that I wished to share with you. I have also had larger examples, too, over the years. I think back and although I used to say it was anxiety, now I realize that it was a message to make a change, and since I wasn't listening it kept getting louder and louder.

Crippling Decision

In January of 2018, I started working on developing a shoe line. I love shoes and at the time was a sales rep, so I had connections to shoe stores and felt very confident that was going to be my new path. Remember—I had written, "What is Next" on 3-17-17? I spent hours and hours developing the brand. Shoes designs, ideas, a logo, an LLC and even the bank account. I hired a designer in LA and paid her $3K to get started. She started researching factories for me and I was set to begin working with a factory in Portugal. It was all lining up except for two very important details.

I didn't have all the money AND I was extremely ill during the process.

What do I mean by ill? I had the skin crawling, sick to my stomach ill feeling 24/7. I could not shake it and I had no idea why. I tried all the things. More time sitting in the hot tub trying to relax, more time walking, music, etc. But I could never shake it. It was confusing to have these feelings. I didn't tell anyone, I kept it inside. I didn't know how to tell anyone. I thought someone would think I was crazy.

On so many days, the feeling was crippling.

Then in March, my husband, Ryan, finally decided he was going to level up his business and needed my help. Both financially with the money we had saved and professionally with writing, as redoing the website and starting a podcast were part of the plan. We had a discussion, and since all of our finances were needed for his business, I decided to stop working on the shoes. It was my decision; Ryan had nothing but love and support for the idea.

Wouldn't you know? The second I said out loud to Ryan, "Okay, we are moving forward with these ideas for your business, and I am no longer working on the shoes," all of the pain went away. The anxiety vanished. Poof!

It was magical to go from a crippling feeling for the previous three months to all of the sudden back to my normal high-vibe-feeling self.

I don't know why it hadn't dawned on me sooner, as two other times in my life I had the same thing happen. The first was when I was a buyer for Target and was struggling with the passive aggressive behavior from management in conjunction with my direct communication style that was not a good fit, and also wrestling with a decision to no longer speak to a family member. It clicked that the same feeling of crippling anxiety existed when I was going through those situations, as well. Once I wasn't involved in those situations, again, like magic, I felt better.

Have you ever had this happen before? Or maybe you have this feeling now. Take some time to connect the dots and see if there is something you can release. I will never forget this experience and the choice we all have to listen to our higher self.

And like magic, what just appeared in my Instagram feed?

> "Never make someone a priority when all
> you are to them is an option."
> —Maya Angelou

Take that "send me a link" person...

Chapter 20

Who Am I?

> "I love myself because I am a beloved child of the Universe,
> and the Universe lovingly takes care of me now."
> —Louise Hay

WHO AM I? DID YOU ever ask yourself that question?

- What do I stand for?
- What do I love?
- What do I wish to accomplish in this lifetime?
- What don't I love?
  AND
- What do I know to be true?

I have asked myself this before but never really took the time to answer it. Maybe I wasn't called to answer it at that time. However, the question came up again when I had a catch up call the other day with Dr. Jyun Shimizu Ph.D., IMD, one of the founders of ISAMIZU. He was telling me about a retreat he went on for his 50th Birthday and they had to sit in meditation and think about that question.

It resonated with me, and I felt it was a great way to end this book.

Often, people make assumptions and don't really know who you are. I find it fascinating how many people comment on how funny I am or how I am not "girl girly" even though in my photos I am all dolled up.

Perception of others. And then perception of ourselves.

I would dare to say I hardly knew myself in my 20's. By my mid-thirties I started to wake up and realize I was intuitive but didn't use the gift. My 40's was the real awakening and all the changes really started. Now I am 50.

I finished this book knowing I have so much more to say. Every day I am learning at hyper speed and it's fun! I am delighted every day with what I will learn and grow from, how I will evolve, and what will be my next step.

But for now, I do have to say, "pencils down."

I know what I know can help others. I am a master teacher, divine communicator, and compassionate soul, who loves to work with people who wish to transform and live their best lives.

We all can do it. I know this to be true.

"The privilege of a lifetime is to become who you truly are."
—Carl Jung

Acknowledgments

When people say, "Life is a journey." I often wonder if they sit and think about all the people that have affected their lives: the good and the not-so-good.

Those people continue to evolve in my world. Some come, some go. But all are appreciated, and words can never express that.

The majority that has helped me on my spiritual journey I mentioned in this book—thank you! The stories you're involved in not only helped me but will now help millions of others.

A special thank you to my writing buddy and fellow bestselling author friend Nicole Russo De Souza. I am always grateful for her writing guidance, support as well as our many like-minded conversations. I am excited for her upcoming journey into this world of being a published author!

A special thank you to my incredible friend and spiritual mentor, Debbra Lupien. She is a gift, and I hope you all can connect with her as well. I am forever grateful for her support, ideas, fabulous readings, and just listening. A precious rare gem in a crazy world!

My beloved spirit team—you all rock! You obviously are an enormous contribution to my growth, and even when you test me, I love ya! Thank you for listening, guiding, and all the other magic that goes on. I know you are busy working on my "to-do list," so also, thanks in advance for that! It's an extensive list, which I can't wait to share someday.

And what can I say about my husband Ryan…one can only be so lucky and blessed to have a husband who listens, supports, and participates in the journey. I realize that is not the case in every relationship, and I am grateful we evolve together! I love you!

With love and gratitude—thank you all for reading this book!
Melinda

Coming Late Fall 2021

Coaching Confidence
Life Lessons from Coaching, Being Coached,
and Knowing We Are All Coaches

**If you enjoyed this book, please tell a friend and leave a rating and review on Amazon.
Thank you!**

Contact Melinda Van Fleet and/or Ryan Van Fleet For:

- Private One on One Coaching
- Professional Speaking Opportunities
- Business Consulting

Email at info@melindavanfleet.com

Connect Further with Melinda Van Fleet:

Facebook: https://www.facebook.com/melinda.vanfleet.315
Linked In: https://www.linkedin.com/in/melinda-van-fleet/
Instagram: https://www.instagram.com/melinda_vanfleet/
Website: https://goodkarmasuccesscoach.com

Melinda & Ryan Van Fleet:
SUCCESS COACHES | PROFESSIONAL SPEAKERS | SMALL BUSINESS OWNERS AND AN OBSESSED SPORTFISHING CAPTAIN

Melinda and Ryan Van Fleet lost their corporate jobs at the same time in 2009. Instead of focusing on their setback, they packed their belongings and headed to The Florida Keys to begin the second act they had envisioned.

Ryan Van Fleet built his successful fishing charter business *Good Karma Sportfishing*, podcast *Good Karma Sportfishing Podcast*, and thriving community, based on the values of persistence, confidence, collaboration, having fun, and catching big fish!

Melinda Van Fleet is a multi-passionate success coach who built her coaching, speaking, and writing on the values of helping others believe in themselves and take action. Melinda believes many women are stuck and unfulfilled their potential. Host of the podcasts *Good Karma Success Coach* and *Confident Conversations*.

Together they make a powerful team helping empower individuals and couples to live their best lives. They strongly believe that if they can do it, you can do it too.

Contact at info@melindavanfleet.com

www.ingramcontent.com/pod-product-compliance
Lightning Source LLC
Chambersburg PA
CBHW020908080526
44589CB00011B/488